ALBERT EINSTEIN
(1879-1955)

The Story of

ALBERT
EINSTEIN

by
GILLIAN FREEMAN

LONDON
VALLENTINE, MITCHELL

By the same author:

THE LIBERTY MAN
FALL OF INNOCENCE
JACK WOULD BE A GENTLEMAN

Published by
VALLENTINE, MITCHELL & CO., LTD.
37, Furnival Street, London, E.C.4.

© Gillian Freeman 1960

*Made and printed in Great Britain
by C. Tinling & Co. Ltd.
Liverpool, London and Prescot*

Contents

In this short biography of Albert Einstein I have not attempted to be accurate to the letter, but to present the life of this remarkable man in a way most likely to appeal to children. When I have come across conflicting accounts of a particular episode, I have always chosen the one with the most colour, and I have freely embroidered incidents and environments to stress Einstein's admirable qualities, personality and genius.

I owe acknowledgements to the biographies by Carl Seelig, Philipp Frank and Anna Frankel, which I have used freely.

G.F.

FOR MY DAUGHTER HARRIET
AND MY GOD-DAUGHTER VANESSA

CHAPTER ONE

The Backward Boy

THE Einstein family moved to Munich on a warm spring day in 1880. Early that morning Mrs. Einstein stood in the beautiful cathedral square of Ulm in Germany, and watched her husband close the workshop doors for the last time. The small engineering business begun only three years ago had been a failure. Now they were going to try again in Munich.

She walked a few paces along the cobbled road, waiting for her husband to catch up with her. There were few people about and Mrs. Einstein felt depressed and apprehensive. As far back as anyone could remember her family had lived in Swabia, this picturesque district of South West Germany, and she didn't know how she was going to like Munich. Ulm was a small city, and it was true that Munich was not much bigger. But how was she going to feel away from the Swabian people? They were so kind and practical, quite different from the other Germans. They spoke softly and melodiously,

9

A*

and had their own dialect. To the people of Munich she would sound like a foreigner. Moving to Ulm three years before had been bad enough, but at least they had had a circle of friends and relations close at hand. In Munich they knew no-one; she hadn't even seen their house, and above all she didn't want Albert to grow up away from the countryside in which she had spent her own happy childhood.

'That's done,' said Mr. Einstein cheerfully, coming up beside her and taking her arm. 'You're not sorry to be going, are you?'

'No, not really.' His wife glanced at the slender cathedral spire which was the highest in the world. 'I expect I'll soon settle down. It was a nice place for Albert to have been born in, anyway.'

'Well, you know the proverb,' said Mr. Einstein jokingly. 'The men of Ulm are mathematicians. Albert's future may have been decided when we came to live here.'

'You are silly.' Mrs. Einstein laughed. Nothing ever depressed her husband, even when business was as bad as it had been this last year. 'If Albert's a mathematician it will be because he takes after his Uncle Jakob, and not because he spent the first year of his life in Ulm.'

They walked hurriedly back through the narrow streets to make the final preparations for their journey. Already Mrs. Einstein couldn't believe that the house had ever been warm and lived in. The furniture had gone ahead and the rooms were empty and bleak. In the drawing-room only the faintest light oblongs on the wallpaper indicated that pictures had hung there, and a scratch on the skirting marked where the piano had stood. She climbed the stairs to Albert's nursery and stood sadly in the doorway. No glowing fire and airing clothes, no toys or cot or chuckling baby. She looked out of the window, leaning her elbows on the wide sill. Albert and his nursemaid were in the garden, dressed for the journey, and the girl was retying the ribbons on the baby's lace bonnet. The young mother smiled. How Albert hated wearing a bonnet! His tiny fingers would tug at the ribbons until they were loosened and he could free himself.

Mr. Einstein's brother, Jakob, who lived with them and worked in partnership at the factory, had been making a last tour of the house; not a sentimental one like his sister-in-law's, but to make certain that nothing was going to be left behind. He saw her in the nursery and called out to her.

'Are you ready? The carriage is here.'

Mrs. Einstein joined her husband and Jakob and the three of them walked to the gate. Several people had come to see them off, including a cousin who was choirmaster to the Jewish Community in the city. The nursemaid stood at a discreet distance while the good-byes were said and the trunks strapped into position on the carriage roof, then she took her place with the family inside and as the Einsteins leaned forward to wave, Albert began to cry.

He's like me, thought Mrs. Einstein, he really

doesn't want to go. She looked out of the rear window, blinking back her tears, watching the cathedral spire getting smaller and smaller as it stood like a sentinel above the trees in the square.

* * *

Life in Munich proved to be far happier than Mrs. Einstein had anticipated. To start with the house had turned out to be a delightful cottage in the suburbs, not the austere city dwelling she had imagined. They had a large garden, and in the evenings and at week-ends they made excursions into the surrounding countryside with its breathtaking scenery of lakes and mountains. They made friends too, mostly engineers who worked in the small electrochemical factory that the Einstein brothers operated for making dynamos, measuring instruments and lamps. And once a week they invited a poor Jewish student from Russia to share a meal with them. This young man was exceedingly clever and entertaining company, and the family looked forward to his visit from week to week. Frequently they gave musical evenings, which meant a great deal to Mrs. Einstein. She was a serious young woman, although not without a sense of humour, and if things weren't going too well at the factory, she consoled herself with music, particularly with her favourite Beethoven.

A year after they had settled in Munich a baby sister was born for Albert, a dark-haired little girl called Maja. Albert was now two, and it seemed he was going to inherit his mother's serious nature rather than his father's jocularity. He seldom laughed, and never wanted to climb over the furniture or play rough-and-tumble games as most toddlers do. His parents were worried about him, for he showed no inclination to speak beyond such first baby words as *Mama* and *Dada* and *Baba*.

'Perhaps he's really backward,' Mr. Einstein said. 'It's a dreadful thought, but I'm beginning to wonder whether he's – to put it bluntly – abnormal. He's far behind other children of his age.'

Girls are generally more forward than boys, but little Maja's rapid progress did nothing to ease the parents' minds. When Albert was three they engaged a governess to help him, and although he improved, his speech was still halting and he wouldn't take part in any of the games she suggested.

'I shall have to call you Father Bore,' she said in exasperation one day. 'You are bored by everything we do. Come on now, how about a game of soldiers? You and Maja and I will march round the nursery and you can be the one who gives the orders.'

But playing at soldiers was the game which Albert detested more than any of the others. The governess was a kind, good woman, but in this sense she wasn't very far-seeing or understanding. Sometimes, when they were out for their daily walks, a military procession would pass them, the soldiers stamping their feet on the cobbled roads to a rhythm of trumpets and drums. Other children were always very excited by the splendour of the uniforms and the columns of tall handsome soldiers marching along in unison. They would try to keep in step, strutting along the pavements, pulling their mothers with them. But Albert always turned away, and on one occasion he cried.

'Those poor men,' he said through his tears. 'If one of them wants to stop walking, he *can't*. He's got to keep on going. When I grow up I don't want to be a soldier.'

The shouts of command which accompanied these parades particularly filled Albert with horror and dread. He thought that to be ordered about was about the worst thing that could happen to a person. Why should they do what they're told? he thought. Suppose one of the soldiers has sore feet, as I had when I wore my new boots last week. It would be better for him not to walk and make his feet worse. Yet he isn't even allowed to rest.

When Albert was five years old, shortly before he was to go to school, he developed a bad cold, not serious, but enough to keep him in bed. At first he only felt like sleeping, but as he began to recover he became bored. He had seen all his picture books and done some simple puzzles. He missed Maja, who was not allowed into his room in case she caught his germs. The Governess and Mrs. Einstein sat with him when they could, but they had other things to do and for long periods he was left to his own devices. When Mr. Einstein came home from the factory on the third day of Albert's confinement,

Mrs. Einstein said, 'Can't you find something to occupy Albertle. He is very fed up with himself.' The years in Munich had not rid her of her Swabian speech, and she still used the affectionate name ending.

Mr. Einstein went to his big, roll-top desk and pulled open the various drawers and compartments.

'I'll try this,' he said, taking out a small silver compass. 'Perhaps it will amuse him.'

Albert was sitting up in bed in his woollen nightgown, watching the door for his father to enter. He had heard the front door close, and knew that having finished at the factory for the day, Papa would soon be up to see him. Albert's brown eyes looked enormous in his pale face, and his always unruly black curls were more tousled than ever.

'I've got something to show you,' said Mr. Einstein. 'Look!' He held out the pocket compass in the palm of his hand.

Albert took the little instrument and stared at it. He turned it round, this way and that, fascinated as the iron needle remained pointing in the same direction, however much he moved the case.

'Why does it stay like that?' he asked his father. 'Why doesn't it point the other way?'

Mr. Einstein explained as simply as he could. 'But you're too young to understand,' he added. 'Don't bother your little head about it. Just play with it. Let's make up a game. We'll be shipwrecked sailors and the compass will help us find our way.'

But although Albert didn't understand completely, he had grasped the principle that something was existing somewhere to keep the compass needle pointing in a particular direction – something outside the compass itself. It was a very profound thought for a small boy not yet six years old, especially for a small boy who was considered to be backward, a slow developer. All through his convalescence Albert played with nothing but the compass. He was thrilled and mystified by it, far more interested than in his father's make-believe adventure games. He wanted to know *exactly* why the compass functioned as it did, and he wondered if there were other things which would do the same. Until now the world outside his nursery had been big and terrifying. The noisy streets of Munich had seemed remote from his safe and happy life, playing in the garden with Maja, walking to the nearby park. Now he was aware of something beyond all this, far more important, which made even his mother's descriptions of distant Swabia close by comparison. He wasn't sure what this 'something' was, but it was to do with the compass and the way the compass worked. The compass was ordered, just as the soldiers were ordered, but it wasn't ordered by a man. The needle couldn't help pointing. It was made to point. It was so exciting and absorbing that Albert could scarcely sleep at night, and in spite of his long rests he didn't look well.

'It's funny how attached he's become to that pocket compass,' said the governess to Mrs.

Einstein. 'It's the first time I've known him to be really enthusiastic about anything. Although I really can't imagine what he sees in it. I mean, what can he think about, staring all day at a compass?'

* * *

There was no Jewish school near the Einsteins' home, but both parents were anxious that Albert should mix with children of all denominations from an early age. The first school that Albert attended was in fact a Catholic one, and although he was the only Jewish boy there he was in no way marked out as 'different' by the other children. He was aware of the differences between his own background and theirs, but it in no way intruded on his friendships with them. Nevertheless, he wasn't happy. His mother and father had hoped that the communal life of the classroom would make Albert more lively, less dreamy and wrapped in his own thoughts. It was not the case. Instead of enjoying his days at school Albert longed for them to end. He hated learning by heart. His questions were never properly answered. He resented having to stand to attention when a teacher spoke to him, and he wanted a reason for every order, some of which seemed very stupid to his precise mind.

'Never mind,' said Mrs. Einstein comfortingly, when one Sunday he couldn't control his tears at the thought that it was Monday the next day. 'I've had an idea to make school happier for you. You can begin violin lessons, and when the other classes

17

seem dull, you can think about your music.' It was her own escape from the ups and downs of daily life.

Albert was delighted. He loved music, loved to hear his mother playing the piano and violin, and thought it wonderful that soon he would be able to reproduce the music himself. The next day his mother went with him to school, and arranged that the violin lessons should start at once, although it was the middle of the term. During a history class, a very excited and hopeful Albert was summoned to the music room. He had not passed beyond the door until now, although he had often heard sounds of scales and simple tunes as he had marched with his class from one part of the building to another. He had seen the music master once or twice, a little white-haired man who was the local *Kappelmeister*, combining his duties of instructing the choir with teaching at the elementary school. His gruff voice now commanded Albert to enter, and he found him-self in a small room with panelled walls and a walnut wood piano which had an ornate candelabra branching out in front. There were three or four music stands and a shelf of books and scores. Albert felt he was entering a sanctum, a respite from the senseless school rules and regulations and parrot learning. Soon he would be able to accompany his mother on the violin.

The lesson began, and before this first half-hour was up Albert knew that his violin lessons were going to be as depressing and useless as all the others. The little master had no time to anwer questions about music and musicians. He couldn't be bothered to explain to Albert why he must do a thing one way and not another.

'Why, why, *why*!' he shouted. 'If I say learn, you learn. There is no *why*.'

It was a terrible disappointment to the little boy, and he felt bitterly cheated. It had been his last hope of finding pleasure in school life, and it had been dashed. It made him more lonely than ever.

He moved up from one class to the next regularly each year, without distinguishing himself in any way. The other boys thought of him as an odd creature, slow of speech, not interested in athletics, and left him to go his own way. Albert was used to school now, and accepted that it couldn't fulfil his needs or satisfy his questioning mind. At least, *this* school couldn't. But as the time passed Albert began to pin his hopes on the Munich Gymnasium, the secondary school he was to attend when he was ten. It was a famous school with a fine reputation, and he looked forward to going, counting the days of his last term at the elementary school.

'At least we shan't be treated like babies,' he said to his mother. 'At a junior school everyone thinks the pupils are too young to act without an order.'

In his imagination Albert saw himself talking to teachers as he talked to his father, asking questions, getting answers, having his own point of view heard with interest and consideration. There was so much he wanted to know, so many facts he *must* know to be able to understand life. There was a law that made the compass work, and there were other laws which now seemed bewildering.

They shouldn't *be* bewildering, he told himself, fiercely. And once I get to a decent school they won't be! He had set his heart on proper guidance at the Munich Gymnasium.

CHAPTER TWO

The Munich Gymnasium

'TURN to page twenty-three of your Latin Grammar,' snapped Albert's new form-master, a tall, waspish man who seemed bored and disinterested by all he taught. 'We will devote the lesson to learning the rules by heart.'

Albert sighed and bent his dark head over the desk. In this first week at the Gymnasium he had done nothing but learn by heart, memorizing great chunks of Latin and Greek, reciting the rules of grammar parrot-fashion with little idea of what they meant. He had considered the discipline at the elementary school severe, but this was even worse and the teachers whom he had expected to be helpful and kind were stern and unapproachable. Albert had already discovered that there were no exceptions at the Munich Gymnasium. You did what you were told, and what you were told was told to fifty other boys at the same time. No pupil was an individual, only part of his class.

So far there had been only one bright spot in the

whole dreary, miserable week, and that had been the literature lesson. The master, Mr. Ruess, was as kind and gentle and helpful as the other staff were sharp and discouraging. Instead of demanding silence he began the lesson by saying cheerfully, 'Let's discuss what we'd like to read this term, shall we?'

It was the sort of lesson that Albert had always wanted, when the class could take as much part as the master, and questions were readily answered. When Mr. Ruess talked about literature, and showed how it had developed and was linked to history itself, Albert felt he really understood how one kind of poetry led to another. It was a complete picture, not a series of isolated epochs, and it was the way he wanted to understand scientific knowledge, too. But unfortunately there was no Mr. Ruess in the Science department.

As the term progressed Albert so enjoyed Mr. Ruess's classes that he deliberately left some task or other incomplete, so that at the end of the day he would be kept in and the fascinating lesson continue as a punishment!

Although school did not satisfy Albert's craving for learning he certainly wasn't idle at home, and was constantly begging his Uncle Jakob to teach him new methods of doing his sums. One winter afternoon, when it was too cold and wet to go out-of-doors, Uncle Jakob said, 'Shall I start teaching you Algebra, Albert?'

Albert sat down at the big mahogany table, and

pushed back the red velvet cloth with its heavy fringe. When he had been smaller, and had needed cushions to reach the table, the fringe had tickled his knees. Now of course, it barely touched him, but he hated to rest his books on the soft surface and always cleared himself a space to work.

'It's a lively science,' said Uncle Jakob sitting down beside him. 'When the animal that we are hunting cannot be caught, we call it "X" temporarily and continue to hunt it until it is caught.'

It was like a game, and Albert's enthusiasm was aroused. For the remainder of the holidays he worked at the problems his uncle set him each morning before he left for the factory, and sometimes even did the same one twice by different methods.

'I do wish you'd play with me,' Maja complained. 'You can't like doing lessons all day.' She was at the elementary school now and thought Albert stupid to work when there was no-one to make him.

'This is playing to me,' answered Albert, 'and I *do* enjoy it.'

Learning was always fun for Albert, never a chore. The Russian student who came each week to dine with the Einstein's had lent Albert two volumes in a series called *Popular Books on Natural Science,* and he was enthralled by the explorations of stars and plants and earthquakes and animals, and the wonderful illustrations which seemed to lift him to another realm. He linked his new knowledge together to form an over-all impression.

Every new fact he learned was like a piece of a jig-saw puzzle, to be fitted into place and bring him one step nearer to completing the picture.

During a summer holiday a boy from the Gymnasium came with his parents to visit the Einsteins. He was a year or so older than Albert and was keen to impress his seniority.

'Of course,' he said loftily, 'you haven't started geometry yet, have you, Albert?'

'We start next term,' answered Albert, and added, 'I'm looking forward to it.'

'Then you're in for a bit of a shock,' said the boy. 'I can promise you it isn't a treat to look forward to.'

'Oh, I'm sure it is,' protested Albert. 'Some figures were left on the blackboard one day last term. I thought it looked terribly interesting.'

'Wait till you have to do it,' said the boy. 'I'll show you the textbook you'll have to use. You won't be so anxious then.'

'I'd love to see it,' Albert said eagerly. 'Really I would, Heinz. Will you lend it to me?'

'With pleasure,' Heinz said. 'It's no loss to me, beastly thing.'

Albert obtained permission to walk home with Heinz and his parents, in order to bring back the geometry book. As he strolled slowly home again his fingers caressed the red cloth cover, feeling the indentations of the letters of the title. It was a promise of all the interesting things inside, and suddenly he couldn't wait to begin reading it. He began to run, which he seldom wanted to do, and he arrived home panting and exhilarated and bounded the stairs to his room three at a time. He flung himself on to his bed, propping himself on his elbows, his chin in his hand. Then all at once calmer, because the moment had arrived, he opened the cover and methodically read and turned the title pages and the pages of the introduction, until he came to the instruction proper. He had enjoyed the little algebra he had done with Uncle Jakob, but now his enjoyment far exceeded it. He was thrilled and absorbed. How could Heinz have found it boring? It was all so marvellously clear, everything was proved, the diagrams and statements explained one another. It was so neat, so ordered, so complete. Where other people might find a beautiful garden an overwhelming and satisfying sight, so twelve-year-old Albert Einstein found the expositions of Euclid.

'He's too bookish,' said his father later on that same holiday. 'He ought to get out more instead of poring over textbooks. It isn't as if they do him any good. His reports are always terrible.'

* * *

His reports continued to be terrible, although gradually now he began to outstrip his classmates in mathematics, and even solved the Pythagorean theorem by his own efforts, long before they reached the point in school. But in all other subjects Albert was way behind.

'You will never amount to anything, Einstein,'

said the Latin master unkindly. Albert went on loathing the gymnasium and the teachers and remained indifferent to most of the other boys. But although he wasn't happy at school, he was happier in other ways. Geometry was one of the reasons. Another was his discovery of Mozart's music, which he found as beautiful and satisfying as geometry.

His violin lessons had been going on over the years with the same plodding lack of imagination as in that first half-hour at the elementary school. Albert played reasonably well, but he was certainly not uplifted by the experience. Then, at one of his mother's treasured musical evenings, a guest played a Mozart sonata on the violin. Albert was transported. It was such clear, precise music. He ceased to see the circle of friends, some leaning forward as they listened intently, others reclining against the leather chairbacks, their eyes closed. He ceased to see his mother in her lilac-coloured dress as she accompanied the violinist on the upright piano, or Maja's red velvet sash. Everything faded before the music, even the sound of the gas jets hissing on the walls.

I've got to learn to play Mozart, he thought fiercely. I'm going to start tomorrow.

*   *   *

Whatever Albert was determined to do, he did to the best of his ability, and he worked unceasingly at the Mozart Sonatas. Sometimes he thought despairingly that he would never be any good, never play lightly enough, but he persisted and even his music master was sufficiently impressed to congratulate his pupil on his efforts.

'You can take part in the next recital we give,' he said. 'I'll see you're included when I arrange the programme.'

Albert was full of pride and happiness. He practised even more diligently than before, and when the great day arrived and he stood with his violin in the school refectory waiting for the recital to begin, he was almost overcome by emotion. He could see his parents sitting in the middle of the third row of chairs, his mother wearing her best hat which had an artificial seagull nesting among an exotic cluster of flowers and fruit. Uncle Jakob was with them, too, although he had said he would not be able to leave the factory. It was the most reward-ing afternoon of Albert's life and afterwards, when he climbed into the carriage with his family to go home to a special celebration tea, he felt close to tears.

'Music's so wonderful,' he said to his mother. 'When I play it or listen to it nothing else matters.'

His mother put her hand on his shoulder and pressed it.

'That's how I feel,' she said softly. 'I'm glad you share it with me.'

*　　*　　*

About this time, when Albert was fourteen, he began to think seriously about religion. When he had been at the elementary school he had been the only Jewish boy and consequently he had had no special instruction. At the Gymnasium there were classes in the Old Testament and in Hebrew, and Albert was very moved by parts of the Bible, and particularly impressed by the code of behaviour and moral concepts it set forth. But at the same time he felt very strongly about having to attend prayers whether he wanted to or not, and keeping customs which no longer had any meaning for contemporary life. His own parents were not Orthodox, and Albert had never been forced to go to synagogue against his will or to sit through Hebrew services he could not understand. It wasn't only in the Jewish religion that Albert found such compulsion detestable. He observed the same dogmatic observances and ritual among his non-Jewish class-mates, and it reminded him of his horror when he had first watched army parades. Being forced to do anything was abominable, and he decided that when he left school he would cease to take any part in the Jewish community. He wanted his religion to be his own, and not to have to do certain things because of tradition or because it was expected of him. He thought it was hypocritical.

He was so preoccupied with sorting out his problems, and with his mathematics and music, that, usually perceptive in such matters, he had failed to be aware of an atmosphere of depression and worry at home. Maja had confided to him that she thought her mother was unhappy, but he had told her she was just being silly, putting the notion

28

out of her head as well as his own. So it came as a considerable shock when one evening at supper his mother said, 'Albertle, I'm afraid there is something we have to tell you.'

His heart sank. He knew from her tone and her words that whatever she had to say was very serious.

'Business is bad,' said Mr. Einstein bluntly. 'We are closing the factory.'

'Closing the factory?' Albert echoed. 'What will you do then?'

'We're going to Italy,' said Mrs. Einstein gently. 'Papa and Uncle Jakob have arranged to start a new business in Milan.'

Albert's first thoughts were selfish ones, and afterwards he felt ashamed of himself. If they moved to Italy how could he take his diploma at the Gymnasium? And if he didn't take it, how could he go to University? But before he had time to voice his fears, his mother went on, 'Of course you'll stay here, darling, and finish school. We have arranged for you to stay in a boarding-house where you'll be well looked after.'

'How soon are you going?' Albert asked flatly. The surprise and the completeness of the arrangements had left him stupefied. For the moment even the separation from his family seemed unreal and impossible.

'As soon as we sell the house,' said his father. 'We don't like leaving you behind, Albert, but your studies must come before our own feelings. Your whole future depends on it and the time will soon pass, you'll see.'

'Of course.' Albert pushed his plate away from him, and put his head in his hands. He couldn't believe that after fourteen years in the house other people would soon be living in it, eating their meals in this very room. He stared down at the white damask cloth, tracing the designs with a finger. He couldn't speak. He didn't know how his voice would behave. At length he looked up, and saw that his father had left his place at the head of the table and was standing by his mother's chair, holding her hand. Albert knew by the set of her lips that she was struggling, like himself, to keep back tears.

CHAPTER THREE

The Rebel

MANY of Albert's class-mates were frankly envious of his sudden change of domestic life. They could think of nothing more delightful than freedom from parental supervision, with no ties except a landlady. But Albert did not agree with them. His family life had always been ideally happy, and he desperately missed Maja and his mother and father. He missed the welcome when he returned from school, the familiar rooms, the sounds of the house as he entered the front door, Maja practising the piano, the creak of the drawing-room door as his mother came to greet him. He missed his mother's cooking, too, her special recipes from Swabia, her honey cakes crusty with poppy-seeds. Now he had to eat the inferior cooking of his landlady, with sausages three times a week. She lit the fire in his room about a quarter of an hour before he came home at the end of the day, and the coals were scarcely glowing, let alone the room warmed, when he pushed open the door of what he secretly termed 'the box'.

At first he had felt rather excited at being independent and alone and responsible only to himself. But the novelty of doing exactly as he pleased soon wore off, and before a week had passed Albert would have given anything to have been able to join his family in Milan. Other boys would have made up for the lack of their own home life by visiting those of their friends. Albert had no friends he wanted to visit. He had never felt close to any of the pupils at the Gymnasium, and somehow the departure of his parents isolated him from them even more. For their part, they considered him bookish and dull, and his aversion to athletics had always made him an object of scorn. The only time he approached popularity was when there was some algebra or geometry homework to be done, and then he was greatly in demand. This attitude of the boys only increased Albert's dislike of communal life. He loathed the organization of the school and the spirit of loyalty to it which was encouraged by all the masters. The older he got the more detestable he found it, and his instinctive rebelling against mechanically learning rules was now backed by reason. So firm were his convictions that on one occasion when, after hours of struggling to understand some advanced construction of Latin grammar he still couldn't comprehend *why* it was so, he refused point-blank to recite the rule in class.

'Haven't you learned it, Einstein?' asked the Latin master ominously. He was a particular enemy of Albert's.

'Yes, sir,' Albert answered.

'Then kindly repeat what you have learned.'

'No, sir.'

The entire class had turned their heads to stare at Albert standing defiantly beside his desk.

'I find it difficult to believe that a boy who has performed the task of learning will not divulge what he knows,' said the Latin master with cold sarcasm.

'I have learned it,' said Albert, so sure that what he was doing was right he wasn't afraid. 'But I didn't understand it. And I won't repeat something I don't understand and get ten marks out of ten for it.'

Someone in the room stifled a giggle. The Latin master spun furiously in his direction.

'Einstein's insolence is no cause for humour, as he will soon discover. No boy at the Munich Gymnasium is going to make his own laws, I promise you that.' He turned back to Albert, and in his tone there was uneasiness as well as anger. 'I suppose you'd prefer to suffer punishment than do as you're told?'

'Yes,' said Albert. 'I want to learn, sir, not learn by heart.' To himself he added, You've failed to teach me. This is your fault, not mine.

'Then I shall take it you did not do the work I set, and that this is some sly method of your own to get out of it. You will stay in after school every day this week, and by the end of that time I shall make certain you know the rule and many others.'

Without replying Albert sat down at his desk.

He had no home to go to, so the punishment itself was no hardship. He had won his victory, anyhow. The Latin master was quite wrong, he wasn't a teacher, he was an instructor, like a sergeant-major. Do what you're told! No questions asked! Well, here was one boy who would put up a fight to learn properly. Knowledge wasn't something to be hurried over and left behind as soon as possible. A lesson shouldn't be just a dreary section of the day which had to be endured. The Gymnasium idea seemed to be to turn out students stuffed with facts like a lot of fat sausage-skins with no variation.

His independence had now made Albert as unpopular with the staff as the boys. He knew he had brought it on himself by refusing to be a part of the herd, but at times it was making his life almost unbearable. He could have borne the days at school if he had had his family to go home to in the evenings, but the continual solitude and lack of immediate affection caused him to be very unhappy. His parents' letters were regular and full of love, and the description they gave of life in Italy seemed a paradise compared to his own existence. Everyone loved music, his mother wrote, the people were generous and warm and friendly, it was such a change from the regulation-loving Germans who couldn't even manage to give a spontaneous kiss.

If only I could be with them, thought Albert miserably. What is the point of my staying here when everything I need is in Italy? I've learned all the mathematics I can from the Gymnasium, and that is the only subject which matters to me. Surely I can get admitted to an institute of technology without a diploma – not in Germany, I know, but abroad where things are different. In Italy or Switzerland I'm sure I'll be able to continue my studies and I'll be with my family, which is where I belong. I'm not a German, I don't think like a German. If I did I'd be happy at the Gymnasium.

The more he thought about it, the more convinced Albert became that he ought to go to Milan. At times he asked himself if he was talking himself into it because he so hated Munich, but he quickly dismissed the unwelcome thought although he honestly attempted to look at the problem from all angles.

He lay awake at nights trying to think of a way of escape. It had been arranged by his parents that he should stay a year, and only six months had passed. He didn't want them to worry or to know that he was unhappy, and besides, they would say again it was in his own interests to stay. No, he would just have to find a way, and turn up in Italy when it would be too late for them to do anything about it. And he could explain so much more easily by talking than in a letter.

Finally, he hit on the idea of visiting a doctor to see if he could obtain a medical certificate stating that it was essential that he should stay with his parents in Italy for six months. It was no good going to his family doctor, so he picked on one whose surgery he passed every day on the way to the Gymnasium.

He was so overwrought with anxiety for his plan to
succeed that by the time he was summoned from
the waiting-room there was no need for him to put
on an act. His pale face, trembling hands and
thumping heart satisfied the busy doctor that this
young boy was suffering from a nervous disorder,
and he willingly wrote out a certificate to the effect
that Albert needed six months' rest and attention in
a warm climate. He advised his patient to go to
Italy, where his parents could supervise his
recuperation. It seemed almost too easy to be
true.

Albert's next step was to see the maths master and
obtain a further statement, this time in the form of
an open letter affirming that Albert's mathematical
knowledge and prowess qualified him, in the
master's view, for admittance to an educational
establishment for advanced study of the subject.

This, too, proved uncomplicated. Albert produced the doctor's certificate and pointed out that
in the event of his not returning to Munich in time
to take his diploma, he might have difficulty in
continuing his studies elsewhere. The maths master
at once wrote out the testimonial, even going so far
as to say he was sorry to lose his best pupil. All that
was left now for Albert was to approach the headmaster, and this he decided to do a few days before
the end of term. He was very apprehensive, feeling
everything had gone too smoothly and that now his
plans were going to be scotched. The Head might
contact Albert's parents, or demand another medical

examination, or even make inquiries and find out that
Albert had had no previous medical attention from
the doctor whose certificate he now held. As the end
of term approached Albert's fears grew, and night
after night he dreamed that the interview was
taking place, and invariably it turned into a night-
mare in which he found himself running along the
school corridors with boys streaming after him,
tripping him up, calling him a coward and a liar.
During his waking hours he rehearsed all he meant
to say, sometimes standing in front of his mirror,
declaiming aloud in his room. At times he felt he
wouldn't have the courage to speak, that he'd arrive
in the study and find himself asking some question
about school stationery or the next half-term holiday
instead.

He forced himself to select a day and an hour
when he really would carry out his intentions. Without fail, he promised himself, he would knock on
the study door during the afternoon break on the
following Wednesday. He decided this in the
middle of a geography lesson exactly a week before
the chosen day, and he was so wrapped up in his
thoughts that he scarcely paid attention to a boy
from a lower class who had come to speak to the
master in charge. He couldn't believe he had heard
correctly when the master said suddenly, 'Einstein,
the headmaster would like to see you.'

Albert remained where he was, looking at the
map he had completed.

'Are you asleep, Einstein?' snapped the master

irritably, and the boy next to Albert nudged him hard.

'Me, sir?' said Albert jumping to his feet realizing what he had heard. 'Now, sir?'

'Yes, now,' said the master. 'Are you deaf as well as stupid?'

Albert began to make his way between the desks to the front of the class.

'Well, get a move on,' said the master testily, 'I don't suppose the Head wants to wait all afternoon.'

What for? Albert asked himself. What does he want me for? Shall I use the opportunity and ask him now? But I haven't got the doctor's certificate with me, it's in my room. I'd better wait until next week, as I've planned.

The study door was slightly open and the head-master could see the corridor from where he sat at his desk. Before Albert had time to knock he called out, 'Come in, Einstein, come in.'

Albert entered and closed the door behind him, and stood before the big mahogany desk with its collection of paperweights, paper-knives and heavy brass desk set.

'I've sent for you,' continued the headmaster, 'because I've something serious to say to you.' He coughed, almost as if he was embarrassed. 'I feel – the staff in general feel – that it would be a good thing if you left school at the close of the term next week.'

'Leave school?' Albert echoed. 'You want me to leave school?'

'I appreciate this is something of a shock to you,' the headmaster said, 'but I'm sure you will be happier away from here. It will be better for the other boys too. You don't fit in, you've never adapted yourself. To be quite frank, Einstein, your presence in the class is disruptive and affects the other students. I'm sure you will be able to make arrangements to continue your education in a manner more suitable to your disposition.'

'Yes, sir,' said Albert meekly. 'I'm sure I will.'

CHAPTER FOUR

School in Switzerland

I T was wonderful to be with his family again, and wonderful, too, to be able to throw off the bonds of school discipline. For the first time in his life Albert felt consciously free, and inspired by his release he told his father he now wanted to renounce his connections with the Jewish community and his German citizenship. Such a decision would be a profound one even for a mature man, but for a fifteen-year-old boy it was incredible. Other fathers might have treated it as a joke, or been angry, but Mr. Einstein respected his son's seriousness and capacity for thought, and he agreed. In this first flush of independence Albert revelled in the knowledge that he belonged to no-one but himself. He was stateless. He was an independent Jew. Later perhaps he would take out citizenship elsewhere, but for the moment he was utterly free, a citizen only of the world.

These first months in Italy were happy ones for Albert. He was on the threshold of adult life, he was with his parents and sister again, and he thought Italy perfect. Everywhere he went there was a wealth of art and music; operas and concerts to attend, paintings to see, superb architecture to admire. And the countryside was lovely, sun-drenched and picturesque with olive groves and vineyards and little hillside farms. As for the people, they were enchanting. What his mother had written was true. The Italians were totally unlike the Germans, they were of a more demonstrative, individual temperament which Albert found sympathetic to his own nature. They were people who acted from their own emotions, not like the Germans, who seemed so ready to behave as if they were pawns in a chess game played by the State.

Albert wanted to see as much of the country as he could, and in comfortable old clothes and carrying a knapsack he hiked through the Apennines to Genoa. He was carefree and high-spirited. Life was good, a secure and happy future had opened up before him. When he returned home his father broke the news to him that the business had failed yet again and he was going to make another fresh start in Pavia.

An upheaval followed. New premises had to be found, the old ones disposed of. The house was sold, and another bought in Pavia. Maja was sad to leave her school, and wept on moving day. The family settled down again to their routine in the new sur-roundings, poorer than before but as hopeful as ever. In a matter of months Mr. Einstein had to admit that his electrical supplies business was still running at a loss, and they would have to cut their expenses even more. He put his arm across his son's shoulders.

'Albert,' he said, 'how can I go on supporting you? You will have to earn your own living as soon as you can.'

Poor Albert. He had shed his worries such a short time and now here he was with a new burden. What should he do? What *could* he do? Had he been very stupid to leave the Gymnasium without completing his diploma course? Would he be able to enter a university? When he had made his plans in Munich his career had seemed very much in the future. This was reality, and a different thing altogether.

With his father and mother and Uncle Jakob he held a conference, and came to the conclusion that he would gain a place more easily in a technical college than at a university, and he needed a practical training. His interests were physics and mathematics and his father was engaged in a technical occupation, so everything pointed to the advisability of his following such a course. The obvious place to study was the famous Swiss Federal Polytechnic in Zürich, and he wrote at once asking for permission to sit for the next entrance examination, and on the given date travelled to Zürich to take the exam. The papers were in mathematics and languages, botany and zoology. Albert wrote his answers without undue worry. He was confident that he knew enough to pass. He passed in mathematics with distinction, and failed badly in everything else. Within a week he had received a formal letter from the Polytechnic authorities regretting that they were unable to offer him a place.

'What shall I do?' Albert said to his mother. 'If I can't go to the Polytechnic, what is going to happen to my career?' The future looked black. Now, he saw, it had been a mistake to leave Germany, but he reminded himself that although he had personally decided to quit the Gymnasium, in the end the decision had been forced on him. He had, after all, been told to go.

He had reached a blank wall. He didn't know where to turn or what to do. He had to decide on some career, but he had no ideas beyond the continuation of his studies in his chosen field. He was even, though without much conviction, considering the possibility of returning to Germany and gaining admittance to some other school there, when a letter arrived from the principal of the Zürich Polytechnic asking Albert to go and see him the following week.

Waiting for the interview was as nerve-wracking as waiting for the examination result. Could the summons possibly mean that the Polytechnic was going to accept him after all? The suspense made it impossible to think again about alternative plans.

Albert dressed with care for the appointment, wearing his best suit and hiding his unruly hair with a grey felt hat. He loathed dressing up, and abominated any other form of headgear. If it rained he would go without a hat altogether. 'My hair dries more quickly than a hat,' he said. He even preferred not to wear socks, but today he would have worn six pairs if it meant his future was assured.

The first few moments with the Principal dismissed any hopes that he was going to accept Albert after all.

'But I'd like to,' he added surprisingly in his rather gruff, guttural voice. He took off his rimless spectacles and polished them while Albert waited tensely for him to continue. 'Your knowledge of mathematics is very extensive for your age, your grasp of the subject quite – er – unusual. What I would suggest, Mr. Einstein, is that you take the diploma which would admit you to this polytechnic without further examination, and I would advise the very excellent Cantonal School at Aarau for the purpose.' He rose, holding out his hand to Albert. 'Until next year, then?'

'Thank you,' said Albert. 'I'll work very hard.'

He didn't know whether to feel elated or depressed. It was comforting that his future was safe, but he found the prospect of another year at school a gloomy one. He had had his fill of enforced learning and militarian discipline. In consequence he both dreaded and looked forward to the beginning of term which brought him nearer to entering the Polytechnic but at the same time meant the return to a life he hated. Nevertheless, he had no alternative but to find himself a room in Aarau and prepare for school again.

On the recommendation of the school authorities he arranged to board at the home of one of the masters, Mr. Winteler, who had a son of his own age. The first day at school, to which he had looked forward with such horror and apprehension, turned out to be about the most unexpected of his whole life. Instead of regimentation, the pupils were treated as independent individuals, and the teaching was aimed at encouraging the boys to work and think on their own, instead of cramming them with undigested facts. There were no class-rooms in the sense that Albert knew, but a separate room for each subject. The Geography room was hung with colourful wall maps and pictures of foreign countries which really brought the subject to life. There was a collection of specimens in the Zoology room worthy of a museum, and a splendid microscope which could be used at any time by any boy. In the Chemistry room, which interested Albert most, there was the latest apparatus. For the first time, too, Albert felt it would be easy to make friends. The boys seemed so civilized and undemanding. When he talked to them he found they were hoping to follow professions instead of going into the Army. Hans Froesch, who sat next to him in arithmetic, wanted to be a doctor. Guido Müller, who showed him where to buy his midday meal, intended to be a dentist, and his friend Adolf Lüthy a teacher. Albert could scarcely believe that all the

time he had suffered the Munich Gymnasium,
schools like the Aarau Cantonal School had existed
too.

He was happy in his lodgings also, and frequently
went mountaineering at week-ends with his land-
lord's son, Paul. He had acquired a great liking for
the pursuit, and often joined school climbing-
parties, and on one occasion spent three days on an
expedition in the Säntis mountain. Albert loved the
scenery, the rugged snow-topped peaks and verd-
ant slopes bright with mountain flowers. He loved
the solitude broken only by the melodious tinkling
of cow-bells, the fresh clear air, the feeling of
achievement on reaching the summit. He looked
forward eagerly to the Säntis expedition, but, as
luck would have it, it rained the entire three days, a
light, drenching rain which did not daunt the
climbers but spoilt much of the enjoyment. Albert
paired off with a boy named Adolf Fisch, who was in
the same class and who shared many of his interests.
They read the same books and discussed them afterwards, and at the time they were attempting to read
philosophy, and had started on a very difficult work,
The Critique of Pure Reason, by the German
philosopher Immanuel Kant. The two boys were so
immersed in their conversation they even became
unaware of the rain. Albert took the more dominant
part in the discussion. He was in many ways the un-
disputed leader among his acquaintances and
friends. His appearance itself was dominating now.
His eyes were large and bright and one felt nothing

escaped him. He always wore his grey felt hat pushed to the back of his untidy black hair, he walked and talked purposefully, and never pretended to anything he did not believe. He scorned deceit and would tell the truth even if he offended someone. His attitude was genuine, not a pose to impress, and his sense of humour belied any suggestion of conceitedness.

'Have you decided just what you are going to do when you leave school, Albert?' Adolf asked, as they rested a moment on the rough mountain road.

'Well, I've been thinking about that lately,' answered Albert, 'and I think my best plan is to be a teacher. I can't earn my living doing research, although that is what I'd always hoped to do. The Polytechnic at Zürich has a department for training physics and maths teachers, and if I do that, I'll be able to support myself and go on with my studies of theoretical physics in my spare time.' He took a step backwards as he spoke, and Adolf cried out sharply.

'Look out, Albert, look out!' And Albert, to his horror, felt the turf give way and himself falling and bumping amid a shower of loose earth and stones down the steep slope. His descent was broken for a moment by a clump of wild rhododendron bushes, and as he felt them giving way beneath his weight he saw Adolf hanging over the edge of the path from which he had fallen, extending his alpenstock so that the white-hooked handle was only an inch or two from Albert's hand.

'Hang on to it,' called Adolf. 'Quick!'

Albert's fingers stretched out and caught the handle and Adolf pulled, and as Albert struggled back up the slope a fresh cascade of loosened earth rattled down, breaking back the bushes which had held him only seconds before.

It was a narrow escape and Albert felt shaken. It was several weeks before he lost the bruises, and he was too stiff to attempt even the easiest climb. But it was just as well, he told himself, his examinations were near and he needed to do all the work he could. It wouldn't do to fail his entrance to the Polytechnic a second time. There wouldn't be a third chance.

The time he might have spent climbing was now devoted to his school books, and the loyal Adolf stayed with him, going over notes, exchanging ideas. Albert took the diploma examination, spent the week in which he waited for the result climbing, and returned to Aarau to learn joyfully that he had been admitted to the Polytechnic.

Three months later, in the autumn of 1896, he entered the Polytechnic gates for the first time as a student, certain that the important part of his life was just about to begin.

CHAPTER FIVE

The Student

HE was a student at last, a proper student. The Cantonal School had been a stepping stone between Munich and Zürich, but this was the real thing. Albert was sixteen, with a zest for learning and a grasp of knowledge far beyond his years. He was exhilarated by student life, the lectures, the coffee parties, the late-night discussions. He was happy studying only physics and mathematics and all his spare money — and there was little of it — he spent on textbooks. He would sit up half the night reading and making notes, relaxing only for short intervals, and even then his mind would worry and pursue scientific problems. Albert's aim was to break down the laws of nature to the very simplest components. It was the compass all over again. How did it work? What was the rule that governed it?

Oddly enough the Polytechnic wasn't much help to Albert. Although it had a fine reputation, the teaching of physics was outdated, and Albert felt he learned nothing there which he couldn't have found out himself from his books. The teaching of mathematics was much better, but Albert had suddenly lost interest in mathematics. The professor, a young Russian called Minowski, lectured in the dullest possible manner, and this was no stimulus to reviving Albert's enthusiasm. But apart from his chosen subjects there were plenty of other things to learn. Albert had never met so many people of different nationalities as he found gathered at the Polytechnic. They came from all parts of Europe, from Turkey, Greece, Austro-Hungary and the Balkans. Albert was delighted to discover that nationalities counted for nothing in the face of learning. In Munich he had heard so much about the supremacy of Germany, and the intense patriotism had frightened and depressed him. It was wonderful to make friends without giving a thought to where they came from. Albert had two special friends, a boy and a girl. The boy was Austrian, the son of a Viennese politician who wanted to keep his son out of politics. His name was Friedrich Adler and he was quite unlike Albert in both personality and appearance, which was probably why they were such good friends. They made a strikingly contrasting pair, Albert sturdy and dark, Friedrich pale, fair and slender. The girl was from Hungary and her name was Mileva Maritsch. She wasn't popular with the other students, she gave the impression of being stern and unresponsive, and she was totally absorbed in her work. She hadn't the art of conversation and never seemed to be at ease. Perhaps it was because in her home in South-east Hungary she had lived in fear of political domination by the Magyars. At any rate she had no time for what she called idle pleasures, and she talked of little except her studies. Albert, equally bound up in his, was happy to be with Mileva, and they spent many hours in his lodgings, poring over books and exchanging ideas, aiding each other's understanding of the subject.

Albert's room at that time was typically Swiss, with a polished wooden floor and a central stove with a warm pipe going up to the ceiling. The walls were white and the windows were double-shuttered to keep out the cold. The furniture was massive but gleaming with polish, and everything was spotlessly clean, the lace antimacassars on the upholstered chairs, the starched white curtains and the quilted bedspread. The room cost him more than he could afford, but cheaper lodgings were hard to find. There were hundreds of students in Zürich and landladies knew they could get any sum they asked for even for the simplest accommodation. Mr. Einstein wasn't able to help Albert financially. His allowance of about £15 a month came from his Uncle Jakob's wife. Albert was forced to cut down on food and new clothes. Sometimes he ate only one proper meal a day, and often made do with a cup of milky coffee and some rolls. He didn't care about his clothes. If they were shabby they were at least comfortable. Appearance had never meant anything to him and so long as his shoes were not actually letting in water he didn't mind how down at heel they were. Out of his £15 Albert was saving £3 each month towards the fee he would have to pay to become a Swiss citizen. He loved the country and he particularly admired its neutrality and the lack of prejudice against foreigners. It was a country to which he felt he would be happy and proud to belong, and he hoped to acquire his citizenship after leaving the Polytechnic.

It was near examination time again, but this time Albert had few worries. He knew he would pass and the question papers would give him enjoyment and interest, not fear. The immediate future, too, seemed safe. Like most students of real ability he intended to take a post as assistant to one of the professors, thereby learning more about the art of teaching as well as having the opportunity for further study. This was the usual procedure, and Albert's work was so highly praised by several of the professors that the way seemed clear for him.

He took his final examinations early in the new year. It was the beginning of 1900 and everyone, everywhere, was full of good intentions and hopes for the new century. Albert's own hopes were high, and as soon as the examination results were published, he applied for the post of assistant to a professor who had always shown great interest in his work.

'You're bound to get it, Albert,' said Friedrich Adler, as he, Albert and Mileva sat in one of Zürich's cheerful cafés, the Café Metropole. 'The other candidates don't stand a chance.'

'Of course he will,' agreed Mileva, putting down her cup of steaming coffee. 'The Polytechnic hasn't had a student as bright as Albert since it was founded.'

'I don't know about being *brighter*,' Albert protested with his usual modesty. 'I *care* more.'

'Well, whatever it is,' Friedrich assured him, 'you're certain of the post. I wish I was as fortunate. It will be some secondary school for me—a poor teacher not respected by his students.'

'You're both luckier than I am,' Mileva said. 'No-one likes employing women.'

'What will you do?' Albert looked at her with sudden concern. How dreadful it would be if no-one gave Mileva a job, and she was forced to go home to Hungary, or at any rate leave Switzerland. He had become so accustomed to discussing his work with her, using her as a sounding board for his ideas, he couldn't imagine how he would get on without her. For a woman her power to concentrate on academic work was exceptional. The other girls at the Polytechnic were as interested in finding themselves husbands as in their studies. But Mileva was different. Mileva *deserved* a husband. She was unswerving in her loyalties and ideas, and a brain such as hers was much more durable than a pretty face and a flirtatious disposition. She was the kind of girl he would marry if he were older and in a position to keep a wife. Friedrich said he thought of Mileva as an equal, not as a girl. He viewed her as he viewed Albert, his colleague, his companion. Perhaps it was because Mileva, like Albert, didn't mind that her clothes were old and unfashionable. As long as she was warm and comfortable she didn't give her appearance a second thought.

Friedrich put down his big white-china coffee cup.

'Let's go to the Polytechnic and see if the new appointments list is up. Let's confirm Albert's new post.'

The three friends walked through the snowy streets of the beautiful town, where the shop windows were filled with displays of long loaves of bread, cream cakes and pastries, cheeses and chocolates. It was a sunny day but crisply cold. In the entrance hall of the Polytechnic the big stove was sending out a glowing heat. Students were grouped round the baize notice-board in the hall where all events were posted — examination times, examination results, club meetings, concerts, dramatic productions — everything important to the members of the Polytechnic in fact.

'They're up then,' said Albert. Something was making his heart heavy, an odd, unaccounted-for apprehension when only a short while before he had felt confident and unafraid. He *must* have got the post. Why was he nervous then? Everyone said the other chap hadn't a chance, that no-one but Albert could possibly get the job.

'I'll have a look for you,' Friedrich offered. 'That's if I can push my way near enough to see.'

He grinned at Albert, but Albert couldn't smile back. When Friedrich turned round again his smile had gone too.

'Albert,' he said, his voice full of incredulity, 'it's not you. The Professor must be mad. He hasn't given you the post of assistant.'

It was Mileva who had tears in her eyes.

CHAPTER SIX

The Teacher with No-one to Teach

'OF course you must go and see the Professor,' Friedrich said, 'and find out why. And if he still won't have you, always remember there are other professors and other jobs.'

'What's the point?' Albert answered wearily. 'The other man was obviously more suited for the post. And besides, all the jobs are filled now. I shall just have to be a schoolteacher, Friedrich.'

Friedrich put his hand on Albert's shoulder. 'You mustn't give in so easily. At least do as I suggest and see the Professor. There may be some error. Perhaps your application wasn't received.'

'There must be a mistake,' affirmed Mileva vehemently. 'No-one could be such an idiot as to turn you down, Albert.'

'Very well,' said Albert. 'I'll go to please you both. But you'll see, it won't do any good.'

He was right. The Professor was sympathetic, but pointed out pleasantly that two men could not fill the same post.

'It was fair competition,' he added. 'You mustn't feel bitter, Einstein.'

'I don't,' Albert said, wishing he hadn't been persuaded to come. 'That's the last emotion I could ever feel.'

He didn't begrudge the job, but he would have liked a proper explanation as to why he had been rejected when both his exam results and his work during the entire course had been better than his opponent's. The Professor, however, obviously wasn't prepared to give any reasons. He hedged round the subject, and after praising Albert's work and ability sat down at his enormous desk saying, 'And now I'll put all that in writing. You should have no trouble in finding a first-class teaching position.'

He wrote the letter of recommendation slowly, pausing to think, even asking Albert's advice on the merits of two alternative words. Then he signed with a flourish, put down his ivory pen holder and handed the sheet of paper across the expanse of desk-top.

'The best of luck, Einstein,' he said. 'You deserve it.'

* * *

Friedrich and Mileva were waiting for him outside the Professor's room. They read the letter and heard the account of the short interview, hot with indignation.

'I don't mind any more,' Albert said, 'so please don't be angry on my account.'

He honestly didn't mind. After all, life couldn't always proceed in one's favour. His turn would come again. In the meantime the sooner he found a job the better, or else he'd have nothing on which to live.

He began to look at the advertisements in the daily and weekly papers, and put his name down at an employment agency which specialized in teaching staff. At first his hopes were quite high, and he attended two or three interviews at secondary schools for posts as physics and mathematics master. After he had been turned down by all of them, in spite of his excellent record and references, and Friedrich and Mileva had both found jobs, Albert became very despondent. What was wrong with him? Was it his appearance? His mannerisms? His accent? Did he give the impression that he couldn't handle a class or pass on his knowledge? He applied for a temporary position at a technical vocational school in the industrial town of Winterthur, a job he didn't really want, and frankly, after his lack of success, had little hope of getting. But he was accepted, and for a few months at least he wasn't unemployed. Yet it wasn't much of a job, just a way of earning a small salary. He had no facilities for research and his pupils were not particularly bright. He missed Mileva and Friedrich and the cosmopolitan life of Zürich, and although his old schoolfriend, Hans Wohlwend, lived in the same lodgings, and he had plenty of opportunity to play his violin in an amateur orchestra, he was relieved when the term ended, even though it meant he was out of work again.

His twenty-first birthday was close, and he felt he should be facing the future cheerfully. Not only would he be attaining his majority, but he had every hope of being a Swiss citizen by his birthday on March 14th. He couldn't help thinking that having Swiss nationality was bound to help him in finding employment. Perhaps his German origin had been against him all along.

His papers came through a few days before his birthday, and he went to Italy to visit his parents, a Swiss subject at last. Before he left Zürich for this short holiday with his family he answered yet another newspaper advertisement. *Tutor in Mathematical Subjects wanted for two boys,* it said. The address was in Schaffhausen on the Rhine.

The letter was waiting for him when he returned, giving him further details and enclosing his references. If the position still appealed to him, the letter said, it was his.

The position *did* appeal to Albert. He liked teaching and thought the chance of giving individual tuition a splendid one. He would really have the opportunity to teach properly, and mould the minds of his pupils. It was the next best thing to teaching at the Polytechnic, certainly far, far better than Winterthur. His employer was himself a teacher at the local Gymnasium, and he kept a boarding-house for some of the students as a sideline. It was for two of these students he hoped to employ Albert.

Albert packed his one small bag again and set off to Schaffhausen. He always enjoyed travelling and the scenery was especially varied and picturesque. Schaffhausen itself was a famous beauty spot with many natural waterfalls, and tourists came from all over Europe to see them.

As the carriage bumped over the cobbles towards Albert's new lodgings, he looked out of the small open windows, breathing in the fresh spring air, delighted by all he saw. The cab drew up outside a neat terrace house with the name on a brass plaque on the gate pillar. Albert alighted, paid the fare with almost his last shilling, climbed the three stone steps to the door and pulled the bell. A few moments passed and the door was opened by a maid with a friendly, plump face and plaits pinned tightly round her head. Mr. Einstein was expected, she said. The Doctor was at the school, but had left instructions for Mr. Einstein to make himself comfortable until his return.

She led Albert up the stairs, and he was aware of heavy woodwork and gleaming brass in every room he passed. His bedroom was an attic one, but by no means gloomy. A big window gave a view of much of the city, and there were pictures on the white walls, and a deep arm-chair filled with cushions. A glass-fronted bookcase stood directly beneath the window, filled with all manner of literature, but leaving space for Albert's own books. The gas brackets on the walls had glass shades, and although it wasn't cold a fire burned in the grate. The bed looked comfortable and the desk a sensible size, not like the postage stamp he had been expected to work on at Winterthur.

The maid left him, and returned ten minutes later with a pot of coffee and a jug of cream and an enormous slice of home-made cake which made Albert suddenly nostalgic for his mother's cooking.

He drank the coffee and ate the cake as he unpacked and put away his few clothes. He hadn't been able to afford any new ones for a long time, and although he liked his overcoat he had to admit it didn't give much warmth. Still, with luck, this job would last and he would be able to buy a new one. And thank goodness he had his citizenship. At least he didn't have to save for that any longer.

He decided to take a short stroll and learn the local geography of the city. He closed the door of his room, but before he reached the stairs he heard the sounds of scuffling and whispering and hurried footsteps, and he was confronted by two boys aged about thirteen and fourteen.

'Are you Mr. Einstein, sir?' asked the bigger boy. He had a shock of fair hair as untidy as Albert's.

Albert nodded.

'You're our tutor then, sir. I'm Willi. This is Louis.' He indicated his companion, who had a more earnest appearance and reminded Albert a little of Friedrich.

They shook hands seriously, and Albert said, 'I was just going out for a walk. Why don't you come too?'

'We'd love to,' Willi said. 'We made your arrival our excuse to leave the Gymnasium early.'

'Don't you like school?' asked Albert.

'It's all right,' Louis said shyly, 'but I'm a bit behind in arithmetic and I never get the chance to catch up.'

'As long as most of the class keep up, the Head seems to think that's all that matters,' Willi explained. 'It's the class that counts, not the boys, if you understand what I mean.'

'I do indeed,' said Albert. It sounded just like the Munich Gymnasium. His heart warmed towards these two intelligent and pleasant boys who were suffering something like his own erstwhile predicament. He was suddenly confident that he was really going to enjoy a job for the first time.

* * *

Willi and Louis proved to be the kind of pupils Albert had hoped for, interested, alert, curious, thorough. It was a pleasure to teach them, and they responded immediately to Albert's brand of individual instruction. Albert was happy, too, in Schaffhausen. He liked his employer and found the food as excellent as his room was comfortable. At the end of the second month there he was really getting results from the two boys, and they were allowed to return to their class for mathematics, although at the same time continuing with their coaching from Albert.

For a week or so this worked admirably, and

then Albert found that the class-master was
deliberately teaching the two boys alternative, and
usually inferior methods to his own. He didn't
want to jump to conclusions, but he observed
Willi's and Louis's work very carefully, and found
that his first impressions were correct. All he had
done, and was doing, with the boys was being
rapidly undone at the Gymnasium. There was only
one thing to do, and that was to ask – in fact to
insist – that Willi and Louis were to be left entirely
with him for mathematical instruction. He could
get them to a higher standard than the schoolmaster in less time. But the boys must not be
muddled by two lots of teaching.

Albert put this to the owner of the boarding-
house in a calm and rational manner. He hadn't
expected there to be any opposition, and when it
came, in a fit of violent abuse, he was upset and
horrified.

'I will not have authority taken out of my hands,
Mr. Einstein. Who are you to question my
decision? You're nothing but a rebel.'

'Come now,' Albert expostulated, 'aren't you
being rather strong? I was only making a suggestion for the good of my pupils.'

'The suggestions come from me, Mr. Einstein.
My suggestion is that you leave my house as soon
as is convenient.'

Albert shrugged. If this was the man's true
nature, he didn't want to continue working for him
in any case. But he couldn't help being depressed.

Out of work again, and all because he had tried to work in his own way. Was there no organization, anywhere, no school or union or club or religion or regiment, which didn't exist entirely in accordance with preconceived and idiotic rules? Try to diverge and you were thrown out. How could people be so stupid?

Back to Zürich again, and the search for work. Albert found it even more difficult than before. He attended interviews and was politely rejected. Sometimes he waited for letters which never arrived. One position he had particular hopes for, a similar post to the one at Schaffhausen as tutor to a young boy. He wrote and was asked to come for an interview with the boy's father, a rich businessman in the best part of Zürich. Before the initial pleasantries were over, the father said without malice, but with firm conviction, 'I'm afraid we're both wasting our time, Mr. Einstein. Your accent tells me what your application failed to do – that you are Swiss by document and not by birth. I do not want my son instructed by a foreigner. Further,' he took off his glasses and held them at the end of his nose, as if examining Albert through a pair of magnifying lenses, 'your features also inform me, as your letter did not, that you are a Jew. I regret that on both these counts employment in my household is quite out of the question.' He rose and bowed and held out his hand.

Albert ignored it, and without uttering a word, his eyes expressing all the disgust and scorn he felt, he turned and left the room.

CHAPTER SEVEN

The Patent Office

ALBERT had never experienced anti-semitism before, not at school in Munich or Aarau, or during his four years at the Polytechnic. He was shattered by the remark made to him by this well-to-do Swiss businessman. What difference could it possibly make if his son's tutor was Jewish? He wasn't going to teach Divinity. Surely all that mattered was that he should be a good teacher of mathematics?

Afterwards, thinking it over in the café near the Polytechnic, he wondered if he had imagined it. His mind boggled at the man's stupidity, the implied conceit and self-satisfaction: I, as a Swiss and a Protestant, am among the best of mankind. To condemn a person because of his racial background was ignorant and wicked. Albert quoted to himself a speech from Shakespeare's *The Merchant of Venice* which he had learned at school: '*I am a Jew! Hath not a Jew eyes? hath not a Jew hands, organs, dimensions, senses, affections, passions? fed*

C

with the same food, hurt with the same weapons, subject to the same diseases, healed by the same means, warmed and cooled by the same winter and summer as a Christian is?' Hitherto Albert had regarded the sentiment as remote from his life. Now it had meaning, and the moral was that every man had his right to live and work as he chose, that all men, black, white or yellow skinned, Christian, Jew or Buddhist, were equal beings.

Did people really hate Jews, despise them and set them apart from the rest of mankind? Here in Switzerland of all places — a country notorious for its open frontiers and friendliness. It was incredible!

'Albert Einstein,' said a delighted voice at his side, 'let me buy you your next cup of coffee.'

Albert looked up to see one of his old student friends, Marcel Grossmann, with whom he had completely lost touch.

'Marcel! I'd no idea you were still in Zürich. Sit down. It is good to see you.'

'I was watching you from the doorway,' Marcel said as he took off his thick overcoat and scarf and hung them on the back of a chair. 'You looked a picture of gloom.'

Albert called the waiter over and asked for coffee for his friend. 'I am feeling gloomy,' he confessed as the waiter went through the heavy bead curtains to the kitchen to attend to the order. 'I am for ever out of work.'

'What work do you do?' Marcel asked. 'I heard

you didn't get the assistantship at the Polytechnic. You're teaching, I suppose.'

Albert nodded. 'When I get the chance. Believe it or not, Marcel, I was turned down yesterday because I'm not a true-born Swiss, and because I'm a Jew.'

Marcel put his elbows on the white tablecloth and rested his chin in his hands. He studied Albert for a moment or two in silence. Then he said, 'Are you absolutely set on being a teacher?'

'Good gracious no,' cried Albert, 'but there's no other prospect.'

'I could give you an introduction to Mr. Haller, who is the director of the Patent Office in Berne. He might give you a job – that is, if you wouldn't mind living in Berne.'

'I don't mind,' Albert answered without hesitation. 'I've no friends in Zürich now Mileva and Friedrich work in other towns. And I'd like a change of digs. I'm fed up with mine.'

'It doesn't do to have the same landlady for too long,' agreed Marcel, stirring the coffee which had been placed before him. 'They take you for granted and no longer try to please you.' He went back to his proposition. 'Are you free to come to Berne, Albert, if I can arrange for this interview?'

'I'll come tomorrow if you like,' answered Albert, 'But I hope your Mr. Haller will employ me. I haven't the return fare!'

* * *

67

It wasn't the next day, of course, that Albert went to Berne. But Marcel kept his word and within a week Albert received a letter from Mr. Haller asking him to come to Berne as soon as possible.

Albert was weary of interviews. They were usually along set lines – age, experience, an apology for the low salary about to be offered, a talk on the necessity of putting work before private life, and finally the promise to let him know within the next few days whether or not he had been accepted.

Albert hadn't been joking when he told Marcel he had just enough money to get to Berne. He really was down to his last few shillings, and his desperation for work made him dread the interview and what he felt was the inevitable rejection of his services. He couldn't believe he would get this job, for which he was totally unqualified, when he couldn't get a teaching post, for which he was.

He presented himself to Mr. Haller as soon as he arrived in Berne. He had expected a narrow-minded official. Instead he found a thoroughly congenial, intelligent and broad-minded man who made it clear at the outset that he regarded constructive and independent thinking as superior to a particular training and routine. The interview was a long one, so long in fact that it extended into the largest lunch Albert had eaten since the job at Schaffhausen ended. They talked not only about the job, but about politics and religion and poetry and many less intellectual topics, such as Albert's dislike of wearing hats and Mr. Haller's pet cat. As they left the restaurant, Mr. Haller said, 'The post's yours, Einstein, if you want it, for £250 a year.'

Albert wanted it and said so. It was the last kind of work he had anticipated doing, but he had no doubt it would be interesting. He would have to sort through the ideas brought by hopeful inventors to the Patent Office, and clarify those which he considered worthwhile. The Patent Office gave legal protection for all inventions registered with them, so that no-one could reproduce, for example, a patent mouse-trap and claim it is their own. The Patent Office kept all records of original inventions and the men who invented them. Quite apart from the actual work Albert was very gratified with the salary and the conditions the post offered. He would be able to live comfortably without worry, and he would have plenty of leisure to pursue his own studies.

'I'll see if I can help in finding you somewhere to live,' offered Mr. Haller, as they shook hands in the pillared doorway of the Patent Office. 'Are you on your own, Mr. Einstein, or married?'

'I'm single,' said Albert. 'I shall only want one room, and I will be most grateful for your help.' But as he walked away he thought, *why* do I only want one room when I can afford more? In fact, I'm even in a position to afford a wife. And his mind turned to Mileva Maritsch, clever, loyal Mileva. Why live alone in a strange city when he could have Mileva as a companion, a life-long companion? They understood one another so well, shared the same interests, had worked harmoniously together for four years at the Polytechnic. It was obvious that he and Mileva should marry. They were destined for one another.

Albert wrote to her that night, his proposal of marriage not at all romantic, but a straightforward catalogue of the reasons why they should become husband and wife.

'Why should we live apart,' he wrote, 'when I am earning enough to keep us both? And besides, we both need the intellectual stimulation the other can give. Do give my proposal the most thoughtful consideration.'

Mileva did so and accepted. They had a quiet civil wedding, and for the first time in six years Albert had a proper home to go to when the working day was over. It was a joy to him to return to family life after such a long period of living alone, and it was equally wonderful to be able to talk over his ideas each evening with Mileva. She was even less communicative than she had been as a student, but Albert was content, and tried to make her life as easy and as pleasant as he could. When he saw her carefully darning his socks one day, he resolved never again to give her the trouble.

'From today on I shall never wear another pair of socks,' he announced. And proceeded to wear only shoes on his feet.

A short time after his marriage Albert received a letter asking him to go at once to Italy. His father was dying. Albert's sense of loss was great and he felt life would never be really happy again. But at the end of the year Mileva gave birth to a son and Albert was thrilled beyond measure. He sent postcards to all his friends, announcing the birth of his 'chick', who was named Albert after him. He hung over the cot for hours, watching the tiny, living creature, his own son. What a perfect institution marriage was, how immensely sad for those who were childless or lonely!

Another happy event for Albert was the arrival in Berne of his sister, Maja. She had come to attend the University and take a course in Romantic Literature. She had been studying in Berlin and Paris, and had now chosen Berne because Albert was there. She became friendly with the Winteler family, with whom Albert had stayed in Aarau, and fell in love with the son, Paul, who was training to be a lawyer. At the beginning of her stay she was always at Albert's flat, but as time went on she spent more and more hours with the Wintelers. Albert was delighted. He adored Maja and only wanted her to be happy.

He was absorbed with his office life as well as his home one. He was greatly amused and entertained not only by the procession of inventors, many of whom were eccentric and unusual people, but by their inventions. He loved the mental-teasing involved in picking out the basic ideas of the ingenious brain-children and in his leisure hours he was often *thinking* inventions. He had an

71

idea himself, and for nights on end he worked at it, first on paper and then in materials, and finally with great pride he produced an apparatus for recording small electrical charges which he duly registered at the Patent Office. He made friends in Berne with a number of people, but he always chose his friends because he could discuss his ideas with them. He did not like to work entirely alone, and now Mileva had the baby she no longer had the time to spare him. Whereas before she would sit and listen to her husband all evening, now she was mending baby clothes or washing nappies. Albert's closest companion was an Italian called Michele Besso, an engineer, who also worked at the Patent Office, but there were others too, and they formed a group, talking 'shop' evening after evening, in the homes of each in turn. This group was the first to hear the beginnings of Albert's Theory of Relativity, which was later recognized as one of the most important discoveries of modern science.

'Time is relative to a person,' Albert said to Michele Besso. 'It goes slowly for one person and quickly for another. The time between meals goes slowly for my baby, because he looks forward to eating so much. But the same time goes quickly for Mileva who has a lot of things to get done between preparing his food.'

In 1905, five years after Albert's arrival in Berne, he published the results of his scientific researches.

'Now,' he said to Mileva, as she helped him tie

up the manuscript in a neat paper parcel for the post and the publishers, 'now we will learn if anyone is going to take notice of what I have discovered or whether I am going to stay for ever as an official at the Patent Office in Berne, a part-time scientist who dabbles in a little amateur research.'

C*

CHAPTER EIGHT

Recognition at Last

ALTHOUGH Albert had disowned Germany when he gave up his German citizenship, it was in Germany that his scientific genius was first recognized. In Göttingen his old mathematics teacher, Professor Minowski, read Albert's newly published thesis on Relativity and immediately began to make use of the theory in his own research. And he was not by any means alone. At the Research Centres in Berlin and Breslau, famous institutions which were among the leaders of scientific work at that time, the name 'Einstein' seemed suddenly to be heard in every laboratory and lecture room, in conversations over cups of coffee or glasses of German beer. An important scientist, Rudolf Ladenburg, travelled to Berne so that he could meet Albert personally, and there persuaded him to take part in the Natural Science Session which was to be held that summer in Salzburg.

In Switzerland, too, Albert was achieving

recognition. At the Universities there was considerable speculation on this minor official at the Patent Office in Berne. In Zürich the leading physicist, Professor Kleiner, read and reread Albert's papers, trying to understand them. He realized they were the work of a genius but could not follow the reasoning. He was an honest and just man, and although he personally could not properly comprehend Albert's theories he felt it was his duty to bring this brilliant young man to Zürich as a professor. He at once approached the University authorities, and found himself confronted by one of those rules which are about as negotiable as a brick wall.

No-one, absolutely no-one, could be appointed as a professor until he had first been a *privatdozent*. This was really an unpaid lecturer. Any young man who had suitable qualifications could apply for permission to teach at the University, and, once granted, he could give as many – or as few! – lectures as he wanted, using the rest of his time on his own research. The reason for the regulation was to provide as many possible candidates for professorships, but of course, being *unpaid,* only people with financial means could take up such a post.

Albert could, because he earned enough at the Patent Office to keep Mileva and the baby, and also because he could choose to give his lectures at times which wouldn't interfere with his job. Professor Kleiner had written to him suggesting that he should become a *privatdozent* at Berne University, and later come to Zürich.

'What shall I do, Mileva?' said Albert at supper on the day he had received the letter. Already in his mind he knew he must follow the Professor's advice.

'Put in your application at the University tomorrow,' said Mileva with conviction. 'This is only a stepping stone. It won't be long before you get the full recognition which is due to you.' All along, since she and Albert had met at the Polytechnic she had known he would make his mark as a scientist, that the path before him was inevitable.

Later that evening Michele Besso called in as usual, and in true Italian fashion insisted they must have a celebration to commemorate the day. Baby Albert, hearing the commotion, began to cry, and Mileva brought his cradle into the warm living-room. Michele hurried out for wine and cigars, and when he returned they drank to Albert's future, an oddly assorted group—Michele, tall, lean and energetic, and Mileva seeming as stern as ever, even on such a gay occasion. She was dully dressed in unbecoming colours, and her not very good health had made her skin sallow and her hair lank. Albert was bursting with his usual vitality, strong and stocky, one hand on the cradle, rocking it, the other gesticulating with a cigar as he talked.

'Of course it is right for you to become a *privatdozent* here,' Michele agreed excitedly. 'You need not lecture often, and once the formality is over you can go to Zürich as Kleiner says.'

'You don't have to persuade me,' Albert said. 'It's not that I particularly want the *glory* of being a professor. In fact I have yet to meet a glorious professor – vainglorious perhaps!' Michele laughed and Mileva smiled at Albert's typical disrespect for authority. 'But at Zürich I shall have so much better facilities for my research.'

* * *

Albert had no difficulty in getting himself appointed a *privatdozent*. The difficulty was in finding time to prepare the few lectures his sense of duty compelled him to give. He was bored by lecturing, absorbed in his own work, and in consequence his lectures were entirely on his present researches and far, far above the heads of his students.

Professor Kleiner paid an unexpected visit to Berne to hear one of his protégé's lectures, and was not unnaturally surprised at Albert's obvious lack of interest in his students. He lectured as if he was thinking aloud, as if what he was saying was a completely unplanned dissertation. It was not really so, but Albert found it hard to arrange his material suitably and sometimes he talked about one thing and then, as if it was an afterthought, returned to it.

After the lecture Professor Kleiner made his way between the rows of wooden chairs to where

Albert was gathering his papers together on the platform. He coughed and Albert turned round.

'Good afternoon, Mr. Einstein,' the Professor said. 'I thought I'd just drop in and listen to you.'

Albert nodded, his eyes twinkling. 'And were you entertained, Professor?'

'Frankly, no,' answered Professor Kleiner. 'I found it too highbrow for your audience.'

Including yourself, thought Albert, amused at the Professor's pompous tone.

'You must learn to talk more lucidly,' Professor Kleiner went on. 'You must realize that your flashing thoughts are not clearly transmitted to others.'

'Professor,' said Albert gently. 'I am not, at this point, very anxious to transmit. I want to get on with my work. I don't demand to be appointed Professor at Zürich!'

* * *

Shortly after the Professor's visit, the post of Professor for Theoretical Physics at Zürich University became vacant. Professor Kleiner at once put forward Albert's name, but the Board which had previously rejected him because he was not then a *privatdozent,* now proposed their own candidate –none other than Albert's old friend, Friedrich Adler, who was a *privatdozent* in Zürich.

It seemed an odd stroke of fate that Friedrich and Albert, who had always been ambitious for one another, should now be opponents for such an important step in both their careers. But Friedrich,

78

in spite of the fact that he wanted the job, knew that Albert was the right person for it.

'If it is possible to obtain a man like Einstein for our University, then it would be absurd to appoint me,' he told the Board. 'I must quite frankly say that my ability as a research physicist does not bear even the slightest comparison to Einstein's.'

Before Albert took up his appointment in Zürich he worked a short time longer at the Patent Office, and during that time he had the pleasure of giving Maja away at her marriage to Paul Winteler. Albert felt overjoyed that Maja should be marrying such a kind and clever man, and he was proud of the pretty dark-haired bride who was glowing with her inner happiness. He felt responsible for her now that his father was dead, and although she had travelled and was quite able to look after herself, Albert felt relieved that he did not have to leave her alone when he went to Zürich.

During the last weeks in Berne, a smartly dressed messenger-boy came into Albert's office and handed him an enormous envelope. Albert was busy talking at the time, and without even looking at it drew out a sheet of elegantly inscribed writing-paper, glanced at the ornate and not easy to read script, crumpled it up and threw it into the wastepaper-basket. He had not even broken off his sentence. He thought no more about it, having, at that moment decided it was of little interest, probably an invitation to someone he didn't want to visit or a request to talk on his work. Some days later a friend from Geneva University came to the office in great concern.

'You were sent an invitation to our celebrations and we've had no reply,' he said. 'I've come all this way to get your answer.'

'I had no invitation,' Albert excused himself.

'You must have done. Oh, you're as vague as ever! Are you quite sure?'

Albert ran his hand through his untidy shock of hair. 'I did receive a rather grand-looking document. The writing was so elaborate I couldn't make it out, so I threw it away.'

'Well, you'll have to come to Geneva, Albert. We're all expecting you. I'm *not* going to let you get away with it.'

Albert laughed, and agreed, and duly turned up at Geneva on the right day, to find that he was attending not only the University celebrations, but also his own inauguration as an Honorary Doctor there. This in itself was a great honour, but Albert further discovered that he was to march in a procession with over two hundred other guests of honour, all wearing their academic robes.

Albert had with him only his straw hat and everyday suit, and that was not particularly clean.

'I won't take part in your procession,' he said at once, secretly glad to have the excuse. 'I'll watch it instead, and meet you in time for the inauguration.'

But the University authorities wouldn't hear of it, and on a memorable July day the citizens of

Geneva were astonished to see among the splendidly dressed academic celebrities — among the gold and scarlet and purple robes — a man in a shabby grey suit, his rather battered panama hat in odd contrast to the violet silk sugar-loaf worn by the Japanese professor at his side!

CHAPTER NINE

Professor Einstein

ALBERT was both surprised and pleased to discover that the flat he had rented in Zürich was on the floor above Friedrich Adler's. Friedrich had now become a newspaper editor, but he still enjoyed scientific discussions and he and Albert took to climbing up to the attic each evening to avoid the domestic hubbub – for Friedrich was married and had children too. There, under the dusty, low rafters, among the stacked trunks and broken chairs and picture frames, the old friends talked as they had done as students, stimulating each other with their thoughts and questions and replies.

Albert was much poorer than he had been in Berne, in spite of his success and socially elevated position. He earned about the same as he had at the Patent Office, but everything was more expensive in Zürich, and as a professor he had to keep up appearances – an attitude of mind he strongly despised.

'In my relativity theory I set up a clock at every point in space,' he said jokingly, 'but in reality I find it difficult to provide even one clock in my room.'

And it was true that he could not afford even the smallest luxuries. His savings had gone on a family holiday in Salzburg and they were now living frugally on a tightly planned budget.

'Whatever shall we do?' Mileva asked one evening, almost in tears. 'I can hardly make ends meet. Little Albert needs new shoes and my own want repairing.'

'You should take in boarders as I do," said Mrs. Adler, who had come up to the Einstein's flat to borrow some mending wool. 'The two or three extra pounds make all the difference.'

Albert was agreeable. Physical comforts meant little to him personally, but he was miserable at having to deny them to his family. Mileva at once advertised, and within days two students had taken up residence. Mileva was never a happy person, but she felt more content in Zürich than anywhere else – unless it was her real homeland. Most people who are forced through political events to live in a country other than that in which they were born feel somehow deprived and lonely, but at least Zürich held many happy memories for Mileva. It was in Zürich that she had met Albert and spent her student years devoted to work which she loved to do. Coming back again was in a sense 'returning home'.

In July, 1910, she gave birth to another baby boy, and she and Albert were thrilled to have a second son. They had already decided on the name of Eduard, but their preparations had not gone far beyond this. Mileva had looked out young Albert's baby clothes again, but the first nights of Eduard's life were spent in a bed made up in a clothes-basket.

'Albert, you must find the cradle. I'm sure we brought it with us when we moved here. You must search the attic, I'm certain it is there.'

Albert climbed the narrow stairs. He could not recall seeing the cradle when he and Friedrich had their discussions. But then perhaps they were so immersed in all they were saying they had not looked around them properly.

The cradle *was* there, just as Mileva had said it would be. But although he searched Albert could not find the mattress anywhere.

'Here's the bare bones,' he said, setting up the wicker cradle and stand in the bedroom, 'but no mattress.'

'Well, I'll just have to make a new one,' said Mileva with a sigh. She had never enjoyed domestic chores. 'Will you buy some flock to-morrow, Albert, and I'll use an old pillowcase for the cover.'

'Very well,' said Albert, who was doing most of the shopping while Mileva rested. 'I can fit it in between the ten o'clock and eleven o'clock lectures.'

The following morning, dressed in a dark-blue shirt of the kind worn by labourers, he walked unconcernedly down the smart main street of Zürich, carrying a sack of flock on his back. Friedrich, on his way to the newspaper office, almost passed Albert without recognizing him.

'Hey – Friedrich!' Albert called. 'Are you blind? Or are you thinking about politics?' He always made jokes about Friedrich's job as editor.

Friedrich stopped, stared and then roared with laughter.

'Professor Einstein, forgive me. I took you for the rag-and-bone man. Don't let your students see you, or they will never respect you again.'

'Why not? Why not?' Albert shouted to Mileva, as he related the episode to her, dumping the sack of flock on the floor and waking Eduard, who began to cry. 'Must a professor always be dressed like a peacock? Does it affect his *brain*? These big, puffed up professors are no more important because of the suits they wear.' Albert had never understood the conceit of some of his colleagues. He had never cared about being a professor for its social esteem, only as a means of continuing his researches uninterrupted. But of course not all the professors deserved his scorn, and nor did Albert hold them all in contempt. His greatest friend was Professor Adolf Hurwitz, who taught philosophy at the University. He was much older than Albert, and Albert remembered him from his own student days. He had not, however, expected the Professor to remember him, and he was flattered when Professor Hurwitz said at their introduction, 'Albert Einstein! Of course, it all comes back to me. When you were a student here you played the violin.'

'That's right,' answered Albert. 'I still do.'

'Then you must come and play with us. We have chamber music recitals every Sunday at my home. Bring your wife and children.'

He had not expected Albert's smallest child to be such an infant, and when they arrived that first Sunday he burst into laughter.

'Here comes Einstein,' he said, 'with the whole chicken run.'

These Sunday afternoons became regular outings, and Albert enjoyed them very much. Having the chance to play again, as well as to listen to music, relaxed and invigorated him. He became extremely fond of the Hurwitzs' children, Lisbeth and Eve, and one day overheard the Professor telling a third colleague of the trouble Eve was having with her arithmetic at school. Albert said nothing, but that afternoon he arrived at the Hurwitzs' house and said to Mrs. Hurwitz, 'Is Eve in? I've come to help her with her arithmetic.'

It was typical of Albert to act in this way. Nothing was ever too trivial for him. He took as much trouble in helping Eve as he did with his most promising students, and as far as his students were concerned he often took them to a local café or back to his home in order to continue over coffee the discussions begun during a lecture period. He would explain the point over and over again if necessary, never becoming impatient, and would go to any lengths to help one of his pupils either in their studies or when the time came for them to find jobs.

When Eduard was only a few months old Albert was offered the post of Professor of Theoretical Physics at the German University in Prague. Prague was the capital city of a part of Austria that became a separate country, Czechoslovakia, in 1924; both Czechs and Austrians lived there.

'Oh, dear,' said Mileva, 'we've only just settled in Zürich. I dread the thought of all that packing and unpacking and settling in again. And for how long? Before we've found our feet you'll be offered something else in another city.'

'I can't pretend I like the thought of living abroad,' Albert said, 'but I think I should accept. It's the money really. Do you realize, Mileva, for the first time I shall be a full professor with a proper salary – no more scraping and taking in students.' He put his hand on her shoulder. 'And we won't be in Prague for life. We'll come back here, you see.'

Mileva was really unhappy about the move to Prague and before the departure she cried frequently and picked small quarrels with Albert. Their contented companionable days at the Polytechnic and in Berne seemed the very remote past. But in spite of his depression about going to

Prague, Albert's sense of humour was not deflated, and as always any indication of pomposity amused him. His discovery that he had to have an official uniform, complete with a dagger, seemed to him completely ludicrous. As an Austrian State official he was compelled to buy and wear this expensive fancy-dress for his inauguration at the University.

Albert was totally unlike the average German professor. At the reception given for him on his arrival in Prague, held at one of the city's most luxurious hotels, the porter mistook him for the electrician who had been sent for to repair the lights. It tickled Albert's sense of fun, and he enjoyed telling the story to the formal gathering of Government and University officials who were solemnly drinking in the grand reception-room. They were all dressed in smart suits and uniforms. Albert had on his dark blue shirt and his hair was long and untidy. The guests did not know what to make of the effervescent little man whom they had come to greet and admire, but who was so unlike the professor they had expected.

However, Albert tried hard to live up to the customs of the University and do what was expected of him. One of these unwritten rules was that a newly appointed professor should call socially on all his colleagues. Albert dutifully began the round, but after the first few visits – and there were to be forty in all – he became exasperated by the waste of time spent in polite conversation, and he decided not to make any more.

Many of the professors were offended and believed that Albert had deliberately ignored them, and considered him either downright rude or stupidly proud, both of which were completely alien to Albert's kind and modest nature.

He made a number of friends nevertheless, and among them a Professor of Sanskrit who had five children and a sister-in-law who was a music teacher. Albert adored the children and played his violin to the accompaniment of the piano teacher. She used to talk to him as if he was one of her pupils, and Albert often said she was like a sergeant-major!

He made other musical friends, too, and in his leisure time he would play at informal concerts in private houses.

He also got on well with his students. 'I shall always have time for you,' he said during his first lecture. 'If you have a problem come to me with it. You will never disturb me, since I can interrupt my own work at any moment and resume it immediately the interruption is past.'

Albert was contented enough with his life in Prague except that he felt he would never be able to make Mileva happy. She seemed to have lost her energy completely and they were at odds all the time.

But for Albert personal problems were insignificant in relation to the problems of science and the world. And here in Prague he had been brought face to face with a problem he found incredible and terrifying – *the problem of the Jews.*

CHAPTER TEN

The Jewish Problem

ALBERT had been a boy of fifteen when he had renounced his links with the Jewish community. Now he was twice that age, and owing to a formality and not a change of heart he was compelled to take them up again. It was in the loosest possible way, but because the Emperor of Austria, Franz Josef, insisted that everyone who taught at a university must belong to a recognized form of religion, Albert declared himself 'Jewish' on the official form, and thought it would go no further than that. He certainly had no intention of suddenly taking up an actively religious life.

But in spite of this he found that in Prague just *being* a Jew made a difference to life.

It wasn't until now in 1910 that he realized that Jews were in any way singled out from the rest of the community in which they lived—not merely by one or two isolated citizens like that stupid businessman in Zürich, but by the majority of the people.

Prague was a very peculiar city in those days, and the entire population had taken sides like two rival schoolboy gangs. One gang was composed of Czechs, and the other of German-speaking Austrians. Both taught at the University, but because of their hostility the University was divided into two quite separate institutions. There were even two professors of everything, who never met or discussed their work. The Austrians looked down on the Czechs and tried to have no contact with them, except as master to servant. It was all ridiculous, as historically speaking they both had equal claims to their citizenship.

When it came to considering the Jews, the Germans were even more muddled, because although they felt hostile to the Jews, about half the Jews in Prague were Austrian and half-Czech. The Czechs, on the other hand, felt that all Austrians and all Jews were their enemies, but the Czech Jews didn't particularly want to ally themselves with the Austrians who already had ideas about a master race of so-called 'Aryans'—blond people with no trace of Jewish blood.

Albert had always kept out of racial and political intrigue but now he found himself in the middle of a web. He did his best to counteract it. He had little contact with the Czechs because life was so arranged that Czechs and Austrians rarely met. But Czech students came to his lectures and worked with him, and in the past such an arrangement had been unknown.

It is hard to fight against existing orders, and Albert observed how Jews seldom achieved the recognition given to Gentiles. His closest colleague was a brilliant mathematician, Georg Pick. But Georg was a Jew, and because he refused to budge from his ideals he never received any real acclaim. He was about twenty years older than Albert, and he died in a Nazi concentration camp when he was in his eighties for the same reason that he was never afraid to uphold what he considered true and just. But in those days, before Nazis had come into being as such, Georg Pick and Albert became firm friends in spite of the difference in their ages. Georg was a great help to Albert with the mathematical problems which confronted him in his research. Almost every day they went for long walks together, and Georg introduced Albert to his musical friends – for he was a violinist too. This meant that Albert could play again, and the pleasure of taking part in chamber-music recitals made him temporarily forget the conflicts between the Jews and the Czechs and the Austrians. He thought these conflicts were absurd, but at the same time terrifying and dangerous.

Apart from Georg and the people he met through him, Albert had another group of friends who were all Jewish, and because of the tug-of-war between the Czechs and the Austrians they wanted to be considered quite distinct from both – just as Jews. They were among the very first Zionists, Jews who wanted a Jewish nation in Palestine.

They took their name from Mount Zion in Jerusalem. But these Jews in Prague thought less about a home in Palestine than about their people leading their own cultural life in art and literature. One of the leaders of this group was a librarian at the University, a gentle, quiet, fair-haired young man called Hugo Bergmann. He did his best to influence Albert to support Zionism, but Albert was convinced that separation was a bad thing. He believed that Jews should mix and intermarry. He thought that anti-semitism was just stupidity on the part of those who practised it, and as despicable as the Austrians' claim to superiority over the Czechs.

'I'm sorry,' he said to Hugo, after a long wrangling argument in which they had walked eight times round the University gardens. 'I'm not going to join anything which adds to this splitting up of mankind. I'm a human being and I belong to the human race. I'm not going to admit to any other loyalty than that.'

'You'll change your mind one day, Albert,' Hugo prophesied.

Albert's refusal to commit himself to their cause became almost a joke with the others. One of them, Max Brod, who was a writer, was so amused and interested by Albert's force of character that he couldn't resist putting him into one of his novels, and Albert's style of arguing and some of his actual arguments were captured for ever on the printed page.

Most of this gathering of clever young Jewish men were writers or artists or scientists, and Max, Hugo, Albert, and a fourth, Franz Kafka, were always among those who met daily in their favourite café to wrangle over the rights of Jews and their true place in the world.

To Albert it was nothing more than stimulating talk. He enjoyed exercising his brain, and pitting himself in argument. He believed what he said but he didn't apply it to real life, and he was sure that although the others were passionate about the cause of Zionism, it was because they needed a *cause*. If they hadn't been living in Prague where the problem presented itself, their cause would have been something else.

It was his assistant, Nohel, who made him change his mind. Nohel came from Bohemia and he was Jewish. He told Albert some disturbing stories about anti-semitism in Bohemia, and Albert started to wonder if Max Brod and Franz and Hugo had something on their side, that maybe it wasn't all ideals. As a scientist Albert liked to see the *practical* side of theories and Nohel's revelations were far from fantasy.

Prague had brought Albert up against aspects of humanity that had never touched him before, and he was thinking twice about problems he had taken for granted. But in his immediate life he had problems too. He was happy at the University, his room there overlooked a lovely park, and he enjoyed the company of the friends he had made.

But Mileva loathed living away from Switzerland. She had made herself almost ill with worry and depression and she and Albert no longer experienced any of their former happiness. She longed to leave Prague, and when, after two years there, Albert was offered a post at the Polytechnic in Zürich, she begged him to accept. He agreed and wrote to the authorities saying, 'This prospect of returning to Zürich affords me much delight,' which indeed it did. At least in Zürich all the people lived harmoniously.

Once again the Einsteins were preparing to move. There was the packing to be done, and it was surprising how much they had accumulated in such a relatively short time.

'What about *this*, Albert?' Mileva asked for the fourth time since she had opened the wardrobe and begun transferring the clothes into a big metal trunk. 'Do you want to pack this too?' She held out Albert's splendid official uniform, that he had worn just once at his inauguration.

'Oh, I'll leave that to my successor,' Albert said. 'If I don't he'll have to buy one.'

'Papa,' young Albert said – he was eight years old now – 'why haven't you worn it often? It's beautiful, like an emperor's. Please, please, before we go, before you give it away, put it on and go for a walk with me where everyone can see us.'

Albert laughed. 'I don't mind. At the worst people will think I am a Brazilian admiral.'

And standing before the glass he put the three-cornered plumed hat carefully on his untidy hair, struggled into the gold trimmed coat and trousers and buckled on the sword. Then, with little Albert bursting with pride and grinning from ear to ear, he walked along the main thoroughfares of Prague, greeting his acquaintances with a bow, clicking his heels together, and sweeping off the feathered hat.

Albert's departure from Austria had not been expected by his colleagues, and Albert had not told them the real reason, which was Mileva's great desire to return to Zürich. As a result rumours began to circulate. One of the leading newspapers wrote that Albert had been persecuted by the professors at the University because they were jealous of his reputation. Another paper said that because he was a Jew he had been treated badly by the Government. It wasn't any more true than the first explanation, but Albert couldn't help feeling that, ridiculous as it seemed to all his friends in Prague, the way things were going it might have been the case. How long would it be before the Government took its cue from the people? How long before the people who persecuted Jews were *in* the Government? It was a sobering thought, and Albert returned to Zürich with an uneasy mind.

CHAPTER ELEVEN

Zürich Again

'I'VE forgotten the solution to what I'm doing.'
Albert turned from the long blackboard which
ran the length of the lecture platform and faced
his astonished audience of students. The Polytechnic had never had a professor like this before,
so friendly and frank and genuine, and without
false pride.

'I'll go to my room and get a textbook,' Albert
went on cheerfully as he walked to the door. Then
he stopped and returned. 'No, I shan't give in like
this. I must *find* the solution.'

And he proceeded to examine the figures on the
blackboard until he discovered the answer.

He loved being back in Zürich. There was
triumph, too, in being the prize of the Polytechnic,
after once being turned down for failing the
entrance examination – not to mention the assistantship after he had graduated. Albert didn't
savour the situation but he *was* delighted to work
with Marcel Grossmann, his old student friend who

97

was with him on the staff. He still felt grateful to Marcel for finding him the job in the Patent Office.

Albert's research was exciting too. He had a new Theory of Gravitation and hoped before long to be able to publish his results. He had had the chance of explaining his work the year before when he had attended a conference in Brussels, and where for the first time he had met many scientists from all over the world. They had included the re-nowned Marie Curie, who discovered radium. She had travelled from Paris and had expressed as much pleasure in meeting Albert as he had in meeting her. She had been partly responsible for Albert's appointment at the Polytechnic, and had written a letter praising him. 'I think that any scientific institution which would give Mr. Einstein the opportunity to do the work he desired could only be greatly honoured by such a decision, and would certainly render a great service to science.'

Albert and Marie Curie had written to each other after their meeting in Brussels, and when she happened to be in Zürich she visited Albert and Mileva. They talked science, of course, but as well as that they planned a holiday to take their children on a mountaineering holiday. Madame Curie had two daughters, Irene, who was sixteen, and Eve, aged nine. Young Albert was ten and both parents thought it was an ideal arrangement. They would be able to discuss their work, and it would be fun for the children to be together. There was no question that Mileva would come. She would stay at home with Eduard. Both she and Albert knew now that their marriage had failed. They weren't happy together. They couldn't trace the fault. It wasn't Albert's success, for Mileva had always wanted and encouraged that. Perhaps it was the constant moving from one place to another, or Albert's absorption in his work, or just that their characters, as they had developed from late adolescence to maturity and parenthood, had grown apart rather than closer together. Even the children had not proved to be a strong enough bond to weld their lives into contentment.

The holiday proved a great success. It was a hot August, and a shimmering heat haze radiated from the valleys of the Engadine. The grass, which in the spring had been fresh and green, was now yellowed and dry. Butterflies settled on the brilliantly coloured flowers and then flew off looking like flowers themselves against the blue sky. Goat bells sounded and cicadas hopped and hummed. The children, oblivious of the packs on their backs, seemed to have unending energy and would have walked all night. But Albert, considerate for Madame Curie, insisted that they stopped towards the end of each afternoon and spent the evening at an inn.

'You talk about nothing but gravitation,' Albert junior complained as they sat, eating omelettes, at a table with a red-check cloth. 'Every time we wait for you to catch up with us we know exactly what you'll be saying.'

'We toss up to see whether you'll be talking in French or German,' Eve said with a giggle. 'Irene won today. She guessed right every time.'

It was a wonderful holiday, and Albert returned to Zürich mentally and physically refreshed. In November, when the new academic year – which always starts in October – had begun, and he was lecturing again at the Polytechnic, he received an invitation to a conference in Vienna, asking him to explain his Theory of Gravitation. Already the news had spread that Albert had produced a theory which was much more advanced than that which accounted for Newton's falling apple.

He was delighted to have the opportunity of visiting Vienna because he very much wanted to meet Ernst Mach, a philosopher and physicist who had greatly influenced his own work and ideas. Professor Mach, who had once lectured at the University of Vienna had been forced into an early retirement twelve years before. He had become paralysed from the waist down. Now he lived in a pleasant suburb of the city, working and studying and seldom seeing anyone except his landlady.

Albert had heard rumours that his illness had made him a recluse, and because of it he was cynical and bitter and spoke sharply and sometimes unkindly. Albert wrote to this renowned and learned man, saying he was coming to Vienna, and asking if he might visit him. Ernst Mach replied at once. He would be delighted, he said, to meet a man whose work was of such interest and importance as Albert's, and would welcome the opportunity of discussing it with him personally.

As soon as Albert had the chance, he left the conference and took a horse-drawn bus to the outskirts of Vienna where the Professor lived. As he was driven through the streets he thought what a very beautiful city this was, with its lovely architecture and pleasant climate. The people were friendly, hospitable and cultured and extremely gay. They loved music, which endeared them to the music-loving Albert.

He found the Professor's house, and the landlady opened the door and directed him upstairs. Everything was spotlessly clean and bright, and Albert followed the directions to a door on the second landing. He felt tremendously excited at meeting Ernst Mach at last. He had read his books and studied his ideas for so many years that it seemed strange that in a few moments he would actually be talking to their creator. He knocked at the door and a gruff voice called out, 'Come in,' and Albert entered.

Professor Mach was sitting in a wheel-chair by the desk which was hidden by papers and books. He had an untidy thatch of grey hair which rivalled even Albert's, and a long, untrimmed grey beard, so unkempt that Albert thought he looked like some old sailor or tramp. He had a large face with flattish features, and there was a sly amiability about the expression in his eyes.

'Einstein?' said Professor Mach.

Albert nodded.

'Please speak loudly to me, Einstein. In addition to my other unpleasant characteristics I am also almost stone deaf.'

This wasn't a very promising beginning to the meeting, but soon both men were immersed in discussion, and Ernst Mach cleared up points in his doctrine which had puzzled Albert for years. In the end it turned out that Albert had misinterpreted a statement that Professor Mach had written, and he discovered that where he had thought he disagreed, in fact he agreed completely. It was a most successful and happy visit and Albert returned to Zürich very satisfied with his stay in Vienna.

CHAPTER TWELVE

War

WHEN Albert received an invitation to work in Berlin he was not altogether surprised. It had been suggested at the conference in Vienna, and he knew that there were plans to found a research institute. He was asked to become the director of this institute, but until it came into being the Royal Prussian Academy of Sciences wanted him to become a member and organize research. What he did not know was that the most important German physicists of the day sent a joint statement to the Minister of Education saying that, in spite of his youthfulness, Albert's achievements were such that his acceptance of the post would be recognized by the whole world as a 'valuable acquisition for the Academy'.

It was a wonderful chance for Albert, not only financially but in the freedom it would give him to carry on with his work unhindered by lecturing. There would be no university administration to contend with, no examination papers to set and mark. At the same time he would be in contact with the foremost scientists and mathematicians, who constantly visited Berlin.

There was only one worrying and disturbing element in this rosy future. If Albert went to Berlin he would have to go alone. Mileva had made up her mind to remain in Zürich with her sons. Although their marriage had been miserable for a long time, Albert was loath to make the step which would end it. He loved his children and wanted to be with them as they grew up, but he had always taught himself that personal problems were insignificant compared with those of the universe, that his own marriage, even his life and his death, were nothing when balanced against the work he would be doing in Berlin. So he decided to go.

He wrote a very simple letter to the Royal Academy of Sciences, thanking them for giving him the opportunity. Perhaps he was thinking of his marriage when he said, 'Accepting the post, however, has encouraged me to think that one man cannot ask of another more than that he should devote his whole strength to a good cause.' His whole strength would be in his work now. He had no other ties.

Albert went to Berlin in April, 1914, ready to devote himself to his research.

'The Germans are gambling on me as they would on a prize hen,' he said. 'I do not really know myself whether I shall ever lay another egg.'

* * *

He felt very much alone in Berlin. His separation from Mileva was now legal and it was strange to be without family life after so many years. Apart from that he was much younger than all his colleagues, and, as always, he couldn't regard the old-established conventions of the Academy seriously as everyone else did. A fellow-professor commented, 'There are two kinds of physicists in Berlin. On the one hand there is Einstein, and on the other all the rest.'

It wasn't only the professors with whom Albert felt at odds, it was with the German people as a whole. His early life in Munich came back to him, his sense of release and joy when he escaped to Italy. Everything German was contrary to his own outlook, the lack of emotional warmth, the patriotism, the love of discipline.

He had arrived in Berlin in the spring. In August the German Army marched into Belgium and the First World War had begun. In Berlin excited crowds thronged the streets, full of confidence in the supremacy of the nation. Albert did not join them. He loathed war.

Many of Albert's colleagues began to direct their researches towards the war effort. They investigated types of explosives and poison gas; some left the laboratory altogether and became soldiers, and all this fervent patriotism made Albert an even more solitary figure.

Life in wartime is always emotional. Death is never far away, people are ready to make great

D*

sacrifices and reason gives way to irrational feelings of love and hate. The newspapers in Berlin were full of Germany's victories and praise for the soldiers. But at home the most vital problem was food. Food was short, so short that soon the majority of the citizens were suffering from malnutrition, and Albert's health was affected, too. He had to spend periods in bed, and if it hadn't been for the kindness of a friend, Hedwig Born, who was a nurse, he might have been a lot worse.

'The one thing that upsets me about this whole war,' he said to her, 'is that scientists are prevented from meeting. Valuable time is being lost every day because the Germans and the English and the Austrians and the Americans are prevented from combining their knowledge on problems which are of value to all men, everywhere, and have nothing to do with war.'

Albert had some relations living in Berlin, a well-to-do uncle and aunt and a cousin named Elsa. They had come from Swabia as long ago as his own parents had, and in the past they had looked down on Albert, the black sheep of the family who had run away from school, studied science instead of becoming a prosperous businessman, and married a girl who couldn't be considered by any stretch of imagination as 'a good match'. Now they found he was a celebrity, he was separated from his wife and honoured and admired by the most important people in Berlin. Consequently they claimed their relationship!

Albert was amused and not at all offended, and he was frankly glad to have somewhere to go for a good meal. He was interested to meet Elsa again. She had been a childhood friend, but it was many years since he had seen her. She had married and become a widow and had two daughters, and Albert found her extremely kind and hospitable, not intellectual but intelligent and imaginative, a woman who really cared about making her home a comfortable and inviting place. Albert visited her frequently, and her two little girls, Ilse and Margot, became the substitute for his own sons. Elsa was proud of her cousin Albert. She couldn't understand his work, but she liked to help him by making life so easy that he had no problems to cope with outside those in his research. She believed that if he had a good lunch and a rest in an arm-chair, he was more fit to tackle his Theory of Gravitation.

It seemed quite natural after a while that Albert should ask Elsa to marry him. For a brilliant and untidy scientist she was probably the ideal wife. She couldn't discuss his work as Mileva had done, but she enjoyed listening to him explaining and arguing with his friends and colleagues, and she was a perfect hostess to them. Albert had not lived in such comfortable surroundings or had his meals so regularly since he was a boy.

He had not forgotten his responsibilities towards Mileva and his sons, and because of the wartime difficulty of transferring money from Germany to

Switzerland he begged her to bring the boys and come and live in Germany, so that he could be certain she was well provided for. But Mileva refused to come. Nothing, she said, would ever induce her to leave Switzerland again. It was her home.

CHAPTER THIRTEEN

Einstein – Zionist

FOR Albert 1918 was a happy year. The war was over and he had spent the summer holidays with his sons, whom he had not seen for four years. Being with them again made the years of separation seem unimportant. Eduard was still only a boy but Albert was almost a man, already thinking about his own future studies at the Zürich Polytechnic.

'I want to be an engineer,' he told his father. 'Do you think it's a good idea?'

'Whatever you want to be, that's the right thing for you to be,' Albert answered. 'Margot wants to be a sculptress.' He felt that Elsa's two children were his own daughters too, and was just as interested in their future careers as he was in those of Albert and Eduard. He took his sons travelling this holiday. They spent some time in Pomerania, a part of Prussia that is now in Poland, and some on the shores of Lake Constance in South Germany, then went back to Switzerland to Arosa and Zuoz, the last a sentimental visit because they had all been together there during that last holiday in the Engadine. Albert returned to Berlin far fitter and happier than before. The war had not interrupted his work as it had done his knowledge of his sons, and he went back to it with renewed efforts.

In 1919 there appeared a headline in *The Times:* 'Revolution in Physics. Newtonian Ideas Overthrown.' From this day on Albert became a household word in England. His Theory of Gravitation had had a sensational effect, and everywhere in the world newspapers ran articles on him, his work, his private life. No film star could have hoped for such publicity as Albert was now receiving. He was inundated with letters, invitations, questions and attacks. 'I dream that I am burning in hell,' he said to Elsa as over breakfast he waded through a typical morning mail, 'and that the postman is the Devil eternally roaring at me, throwing new bundles of letters at my head because I have not yet answered the old ones.' He could scarcely venture into the street without having an autograph book and a pen thrust into his hands. To his astonishment he learned that various countries were 'tailoring' him to fit their needs. The British ignored his German ancestry, the Germans ignored his Jewish blood. Albert, who worked for all mankind, was quite outside the battle and observed its progress with his usual good humour.

He did realize, however, that he had been forced into a position of responsibility. Any person in the public eye owes it to his fellow-men to use his influence for the general good. Albert knew that whatever he said in public would be reported in the newspapers, and he decided that whenever he could he would try to further the cause of peace.

'My pacifism is an instinctive feeling,' he said on one occasion, 'a feeling that possesses me because the murder of men is disgusting. My attitude is not derived from any intellectual theory but is based on my deepest antipathy to every kind of cruelty and hatred.'

Albert still managed to keep his private life separate from his busy public one, and he was able to bring his mother from Italy to stay with him. She was very old now, and no longer strong, and she was overjoyed to be with her son and to stay in his spacious and beautifully furnished flat in Berlin. They talked for hours about the days when they lived in Munich and Milan, and old Mrs. Einstein asked countless questions about Maja and her husband Paul, about young Albert and Eduard and Mileva, and about Albert's work. It was a sad as well as a happy time. The excitement of the journey and seeing Albert and her niece, Elsa, meeting Ilse and Margot for the first time, all made her tired, and Albert couldn't help comparing this frail old woman with the beautiful and active mother he remembered, busy in the running of her home, cooking, looking after her husband, playing the piano, keeping them all cheerful even when the business was doing badly.

While she was staying in Berlin, Albert's mother became seriously ill, and after a short while she died. Her death upset Albert very much, and it came at a time when he was also greatly disturbed by news in the outside world. The happy summer with his sons seemed as remote as his childhood. The whole year became fixed in his memory as a tragic and important one—the year in which he lost his mother and actively took up the cause of Zionism.

The war might be over, but anti-semitism had not declined in Germany. It had spread. And to make matters worse the various groups of Jews were despising the others, the long-established families shunning the more recent immigrants, and in turn the Jews from Hungary, Poland and even Austria were held in scorn and ridicule. Albert was horrified. It seemed to him that there was now a seed of destruction within the Jewish community as well as external attack. He had realized that with his fame he had acquired responsibility. Now he took it a step further. That responsibility was to his own people, to the Jews.

Albert had always had doubts about Zionism. Back in Prague he had argued fiercely against it. He didn't believe in nationalism, it led to war and the wrong sorts of feeling. If Palestine was to become a new nation for Jews, would it really help mankind? He thought, too, that Palestine wasn't large enough, and he envisaged trouble with the Arabs who lived there. But now he felt that in spite of the difficulties that were bound to arise, and the reasons against it, a national home was the only solution to the Jewish problem. The British Government had said it would support the plan, and all over the world Jews were uniting in their efforts to achieve the goal, to have their *own* country, not to be for ever the rather unwelcome visitors in those belonging to other people.

At that time there was an appeal for money to build a university in Jerusalem, and to this Albert felt he could give his entire heart. He had been horrified at the rejection of Jewish students and teachers at some European universities, and he felt it was essential for them to have their own where they would be free. The leader of the Zionist movement was a professor of chemistry at Manchester University. His name was Chaim Weizmann, and Albert got in touch with him.

Once a well-known person stops sitting on the fence and takes up an active cause there is bound to be opposition. And sure enough an organization was promptly formed solely to challenge Albert— an anti-Einstein society. It paid anyone who would heckle Albert at meetings or write against him in newspapers. It used posters to draw new recruits, and it even attempted to enlist a few Jews as a kind of camouflage.

It made life very difficult for Albert. He found that not all his so-called friends lived up to that name. Probably the last thing the anti-Einstein people intended was that they should give him more notoriety, but that was the case. Such conflicts raged about him that he received even more invitations than usual to lecture abroad, and he visited London and Holland, and in 1921 he returned to Prague and astonished everyone at an important scientific discussion by playing a Mozart sonata instead of making a speech.

He visited Vienna too, and found that his old friend Friedrich Adler was in prison for life, having assassinated one of the heads of Government by shooting him during a dinner in a big hotel. Albert remembered how Friedrich's father had sent his son to Zürich to avoid politics. It was ironical that this was how Friedrich's life had turned out.

Albert stayed with a well-known physicist and his wife, Paul and Tatiana Ehrenfest, who were old friends, and he was amused at Tatiana's concern for his appearance. She sent his second pair of trousers to be pressed so that he should look presentable at a lecture he was giving – a lecture which was to be attended by over three thousand people – and in error he wore the unpressed pair! She even bought him a pair of bedroom slippers, thinking he must have left his own at home, but she met him the next morning, barefooted in the hall.

'Didn't you find the slippers in your room, Albert?' she asked.

'They are entirely unnecessary ballast,' he replied – but he remembered to wear them to please her during the rest of his stay.

Albert returned to Berlin, where he was more of a public figure than ever. Likenesses of him appeared in newspaper cartoons and the name Einstein came to mean anyone who produced an idea that few could understand, but gained world-wide admiration for it.

Not long after he arrived home he received an invitation from Chaim Weizmann to go with him to the United States and raise more money for the Hebrew University. American Jews were notoriously rich, and Chaim Weizmann thought that Albert's fame as a scientist would encourage them to give freely to an educational cause which he supported.

Albert was willing and anxious to go. It was immensely important for the Jewish people and he wanted to contribute something else to the world besides scientific discoveries. This time he took Elsa with him. Her companionship and thoughtfulness had become essential to him, and although he jokingly complained that on journeys she treated him like a piece of furniture that needed constant dusting, he didn't want to make another trip without her—especially such a long one as this.

The journey itself was a restful holiday—nothing but the gentle throb of the ship's engines and the vast Atlantic. Albert liked to stand on deck watching the V of foam cutting through the dark waves at the stern of the ship, the gulls which had followed them since they had left dock flying overhead, and settling occasionally on the white-painted upper-works. The weather was good, no storms or choppy seas, and Elsa and Albert really relaxed, stretching out on canvas chairs and watching the other passengers playing deck games, the ever-attendant stewards in their white coats bringing them rugs if it became cool, and drinks and sandwiches and magazines.

They passed the Statue of Liberty at five o'clock in the morning. Albert rose at four so that he would be bound to see it. He was excited about visiting America, he believed it really was the 'new' world, where people of all creeds and nationalities could live tolerantly side by side. He wasn't going to miss the Statue of Liberty, the symbol of true liberty which he had not found in Prague or Berlin.

They docked at seven, but it was nearly nine before the passengers disembarked. There were formalities on board, passports, customs, not to mention breakfast. Albert and Elsa saw that their luggage was under control and then prepared to go ashore.

'Hi there, Professor,' a voice called, and as Albert turned in its direction a flash bulb exploded.

'Look this way, Prof,' called a second voice and the light flashed again.

Albert was used to publicity, to being photographed and questioned by reporters, but he had never in his life been faced by so many Press photographers and such a barrage of questions.

'I feel like a prima donna,' he said to Elsa. That was written down on the shorthand pads, too.

'Is it true only twelve people understand the Theory of Relativity?'

'Every physicist who attempts to understand can do so. All my students in Berlin understood it.'

'Why are so many thousands of people crazy about a theory they can't understand?'

'That is a problem of psychologists.'

And so it went on.

'Well, gentlemen,' said Albert at last, 'I hope I have passed my examination.'

'Say, Mrs. Einstein,' called out a reporter, 'do you understand your husband's work?'

'Oh, no,' said Elsa, 'although he's always explaining it to me. But it's not necessary for my happiness.'

Finally they were allowed to go. Police cleared a path through the huge crowd, and Albert, his pipe in one hand and his violin case in the other, set foot on American soil.

Chaim Weizmann had been right when he thought that Albert's presence would help the appeal. Albert was mobbed wherever they went. He was frankly astonished at his success, and it was certainly remarkable that a scientist should arouse such fervour. His personality, his cause, his fame, all combined to create the enthusiasm. When he was asked how he felt about the impact he was making, he said, 'The impression cannot be very elevating when I remember that a victorious boxer is received with still greater enthusiasm.' And on another occasion he commented, 'The ladies in

New York want to have a new style every year —
this year the fashion is Relativity.'

Meetings had been organized by Zionists in
towns and cities throughout the United States.
Albert usually sat near Chaim Weizmann, and
sometimes he spoke after him. He did not try to
obtain any personal triumph, and once, when he
was asked to speak, he said only, 'Your leader, Dr.
Weizmann, has spoken, and he has spoken very
well for us all. Follow him and you will do well.
That is all I have to say.'

Everywhere they travelled people were
reminded of the great services that the Jews had
rendered — as ordinary citizens and soldiers, and as
politicians, scientists, writers and musicians.
American Jews felt proud that Einstein was a Jew,
proud of their people, proud that they were Jews
too. In Cleveland, Ohio, all the Jewish business-
men closed their offices and shops and marched
with him in a parade from the station to the City
Hall. The whole tour was a remarkable, almost a
unique success. And for Albert personally it was a
success too. America had not let him down. He
was struck, as he had hoped to be, by the energy
and vitality of the people, the zest for learning, the
lack of prejudice.

'Much is to be expected from American youth,'
he said, as he took a puff at his much-loved old
briar pipe. He sought for a comparison and found
it close at hand. 'It's like a pipe, as yet unsmoked,
young and fresh.'

America was a country in which he felt that one day he might happily live. He was convinced now that his stay in Germany was not permanent – that from now on no Jew could or should consider Germany his home.

'I'm glad,' said Albert simply, 'that I accepted Weizmann's invitation.'

CHAPTER FOURTEEN

Travel and the Nobel Prize

ALBERT seemed destined to travel. No sooner was he home from America than he received an invitation to go to England. Lord Haldane, who had been the Minister for War and was an amateur scientist, was responsible for this. He wanted Albert to give some lectures and meet British scientists. He had another motive too. He thought it was about time England and Germany stopped thinking of each other as enemies. There was no point in carrying on their wartime hatred of each other, and it seemed to Lord Haldane that a free exchange of cultural and scientific ideas was the thin end of the wedge – a belief wholeheartedly shared by Albert.

He stayed in Lord Haldane's house, and found London with its centuries-old buildings and sedate taxi-cabs very calm after the hustle of his American tour. Englishmen are not given to mobbing, and Albert was amused at the contrast between his two visits. Nevertheless, although there was no frenzied autograph-hunting, Albert's presence in England caused plenty of interest and excitement, particularly among scholars and men of letters. Lord Haldane gave dinner and luncheon parties so that Albert could meet as many eminent people as possible. The Prime Minister, Mr. Lloyd George, came to one of them, and Bernard Shaw, who in his way had made as big a stir as Albert, to another. Albert was a good match for the Irish playwright's sharp and witty tongue.

'Tell me, my dear Einstein,' said Bernard Shaw, 'do you really understand what you write?'

Albert smiled. 'As much as you understand *your* writings, dear Bernard.' Such remarks were seized upon by reporters and read the next morning in newspapers all over the world.

The Archbishop of Canterbury had heard that Albert was in England, and had written to Lord Haldane asking for an introduction. Lord Haldane was delighted to oblige, and asked the Archbishop to dine. He sat him next to Albert at the table, and the two men were soon deep in conversation. During the fish course the Archbishop suddenly asked bluntly, 'Tell me, what effect does your Theory of Relativity have on Religion?'

'None,' Albert answered without hesitation. 'Relativity is a purely scientific matter and has nothing to do with Religion.'

And he added, 'The less knowledge a scholar possesses the farther he feels from God. But the greater his knowledge the nearer is his approach to God.'

This question of Relativity puzzled most people, not only the Archbishop. An American offered a prize of five thousand dollars for the best essay on the theory, stipulating that it must not be more than three thousand words long – and that isn't much more than twelve average-sized typed pages. The prize was such a generous one that the response was overwhelming. Albert observed dryly, 'I am the only one in my entire circle of friends who is not participating. I don't believe I have the ability to accomplish the task.' The prize was won by an Irishman who worked in a Patent Office, which was a coincidence as it was in a Patent Office that the theory first began.

Among Albert's acquaintances in Berlin was the Minister of Foreign Affairs, Walther Rathenau. He was a wise and pleasant man, a Jew, and Albert liked and respected him. Quite unexpectedly, in June, 1922, he was murdered by a group of students who opposed the Government. Albert was shocked and distressed, and although the Government made the day of the funeral one of national mourning, there was rioting in the streets and wild anti-Government demonstrations. A rumour spread that Albert was next on the murderers' list. He thought it was nonsense and said so, and the police, who were anxious to avoid panic, said the same thing. But Albert's friends and family were worried and uneasy, and persuaded him not to make too many public appearances. Elsa was particularly glad when Albert's travelling began again, although only a short while before she had said she wished he need never again leave home.

This time he was going to France. Such a move was extremely unpopular in Germany – not with the Government or scientists, who saw only good in such an arrangement – but with the man-in-the-street who still considered France as an enemy in spite of the fact that the war had been over for four years. There was a similar feeling in France about entertaining a German. Albert's train to Paris was taken into a siding because at the main station a shouting crowd of students was waiting for him. The police feared it was hostile and that an attempt might be made on Albert's life. In reality it was a gathering of admirers who had come to welcome him!

Albert gave a public lecture at the Collège de France in Paris, and his old and dear friend Madame Curie was among the large audience. Albert enjoyed going to France, but he loathed the political aspects of his visit. It was the height of blind stupidity for the scientists who attended his lecture to be chastised in the Press for listening to a man 'whose people killed our sons'.

On his return from Paris Albert found an invitation from Zürich awaiting him. He would have liked to have gone to the city he considered his home, but he was tired.

'Tell your students that as a Zürich old boy I was

touched and pleased by their invitation,' he wrote, 'but I so urgently need a little respite. You must not take it amiss and say *He went to Paris but did not come to us.*'

But Albert wasn't allowed to rest for long – nor did he really want to. He enjoyed seeing the world and was particularly looking forward to his next trip. He felt he knew Europe and the West, and now he was going in a different direction – to the Far East. He had been asked to visit China and Japan and he was going to take the opportunity of seeing Palestine too.

It was an exciting time for Albert and Elsa, the long sea journey, and then, as their ship drew alongside Shanghai pier, the astonishing sound of children's voices singing the German National Song, *Deutschland, Deutschland, über alles.* It was the pupils and teachers of the German school who had turned out in force to welcome their great compatriot. It was only the first of many demonstrations to honour him, both as a German and as a scientist, and the honours included a private audience with China's Empress. While he was in this country he learned of an honour nearer home. The Swedish Academy had awarded him the Nobel Prize for Physics for his Quantum Theory – perhaps the greatest tribute of all.

Five days later Albert went to Japan and stayed there for four months. He loved the country and the gentle, polite people who seemed so moderate and relaxed in comparison with the Europeans among whom he lived. He admired the Japanese love of art and theatre, and was amazed when he discovered that whole families made a visit to a concert hall a full day's outing, even taking a picnic with them so that they need not interrupt their listening. This was real musical appreciation.

Albert's lectures were always attended by hundreds of students, and as they could not understand German, an interpreter translated each sentence as soon as it was uttered. The first lecture took four hours and Albert was quite upset.

'Those poor people,' he said to Elsa afterwards, 'sitting there all that time. I'll have to cut it down.'

So on the next occasion he condensed it by an hour and a half, and felt very pleased with himself for having been more concise, for he had left out nothing of importance. That same evening he took a train to the next city on his tour. Opposite him were two men, and after staring at him and obviously recognizing him, they began to whisper. Albert knew they must be discussing him and since it was so unlike the normal good manners he had come to associate with the Japanese people, he became worried. At last he could bear it no longer. He leant forward and interrupted the whispering.

'Please tell me truthfully if there is something the matter?'

The two men looked uncomfortable, and then one of them said, 'Professor Einstein, do forgive us. It is just that your first lecture lasted four hours, and the people who arranged the one you gave this afternoon are very offended because this time you only spoke for two and a half.'

* * *

Albert went to Palestine in February. Palestine was then administered by Britain under 'Mandate' for the League of Nations. Albert was invited by the High Commissioner, Sir Herbert Samuel, to stay with him. Sir Herbert was an English Jew and had a most difficult job. He had to keep the peace between the Jews and the Arabs, but because he was a Jew himself the Arabs were suspicious of him. He was particularly careful not to favour the Jews – and that made him unpopular with *them*.

Although Albert had worked hard for the Zionists, he wasn't popular with everyone in Palestine. The Orthodox Jews resented his not being in the least Orthodox himself, and the most patriotic ones despised him for not coming to live and work among them.

Albert wanted to see all aspects of the country. He went to the brand new city of Tel-Aviv, and to the *kibbutzim* at Dagania. The head of the community there was a girl of twenty-two, by the name of Miriam, and Albert recognized her as a little girl he had known in Prague. He asked her a great many questions as they sat in an orange grove cultivated by the workers in the *kibbutz*, Albert seated at a small wooden table, the vase of poppies before him brilliantly scarlet against the blue sky,

Miriam sitting cross-legged on the ground. Albert was impressed by the devotion and hard work and self-sacrifice of the Jews on the *kibbutz,* where a labourer and a schoolmaster could live side by side working for the same ideals.

Albert and Elsa travelled by sea from Palestine to France, and then went to Spain. Albert loved the scenery and the architecture, and the wonderful paintings in the art galleries. He met and talked to people of all kinds, and was privileged to meet the King. Life seemed like a dream.

'Let's enjoy it,' he said to Elsa, 'before we wake up.'

'Only one more stop now,' Elsa answered, for she was anxious to be at home again. And in July she accompanied him to Gothenburg, in Sweden, where he gave a lecture and received the Nobel Prize award. This considerable sum of money he sent to Mileva, to make life easier for her and the boys.

When he was settled again in Berlin, with Elsa, Margot and Ilse, and any thought of travel far from his mind, Albert was astonished to read in his newspaper that he was expected in Moscow at the end of September to lecture on Relativity. This was completely untrue. He had not been invited to Russia, nor did he have any intention of going. This odd piece of false information was followed in October by an announcement that he had left for Moscow – two weeks later a third paragraph said he was arriving in Petrograd (now Leningrad) shortly, and yet again, a week later, this was verified by a statement which said he was staying in Petrograd for three days. Thus he made a fictitious journey to a country he never visited in his life, and received many letters threatening to kill him for being a Bolshevist.

No attempt was made on Albert's life this time, but eighteen months later a strange and distraught woman rushed into the block of flats where he lived and bumped headlong into Margot, who happened to be in the hall. She had a feeling this mad-looking creature was on her way to see Albert and she ran to the nearest telephone box and told the maid to say her stepfather was out. Then she telephoned the police. They arrived in a matter of minutes, and discovered that Margot's hunch had been correct. The woman did want to see Albert. She wanted to shoot him.

She was taken to the police station and there the whole story came out. This was no political assassination. The poor woman had escaped from a lunatic asylum and was convinced that Albert was really a man called Asev, a spy, who had been in love with her and deserted her.

Albert was most concerned and hurried to the police station to see if he could help.

'What have you actually got against me?' he asked, after seeing the now unloaded revolver which had been removed from her handbag.

'Against you?' she said, staring at him coldly. 'Absolutely nothing. Asev had a much longer nose.'

Albert couldn't help feeling that after all the letters he had had in which the writers had sworn to shoot him, it was ironic that this pathetic woman was the only person who had actually tried to do it.

E

CHAPTER FIFTEEN

Half-Century

SCARCELY a day passed without some invitation arriving for Albert to give a lecture or accept a new post. Some of them were quite alluring and attractive, but for the time being Albert was happy in Berlin. After all his travelling he was glad to settle into a working routine, and the conditions for his research at the Academy were ideal. He did, however, decide to accept an associate professorship in the old Dutch town of Leyden and commute between the two places. Paul Ehrenfest had come from Vienna to be Professor of Physics at the University, and so once again Albert was able to take advantage of Tatiana's hospitality. She always had a meal ready for him and he was able to come and go as he pleased, just as if it was his own house.

'What more can a man want?' he said, sitting down to a simple but delicious supper. 'Plus a violin, a bed, a table and a chair?'

Tatiana loved having Albert to stay, although

she complained that she never had the chance to talk to him.

'We will go for a walk together now,' said Albert, 'and talk until our throats are too sore to go on.'

They started out, but before long the word went round that Professor Einstein was walking in the town, and immediately reporters and photographers arrived to see if they could get some new angle or remark for their various newspapers. Albert tried to send them away but they refused to leave, following behind and dodging in front as Albert and Tatiana tried to continue their walk.

'It's impossible to have any intelligent conversation like this,' Tatiana almost shouted in her annoyance. 'Albert, *do* get rid of them.'

'Go away,' said Albert, waving his arms. 'No more today.'

'Please, Professor,' said a small voice at his side, 'won't you answer just a few questions?' The neatly-dressed woman who had spoken looked tearful and Albert, who hated to refuse anyone anything, nearly softened.

Tatiana tugged at his arm. 'Come *on*, Albert.'

'Please,' the woman begged, and tears actually came into her eyes, 'I've come all the way from Germany in the hope of an interview with you. I even travelled with you on the same train but I didn't have a chance to speak to you. I'm a widow and I depend on my journalism to keep my children.'

'How many children have you?' asked Albert.

131

'Three.'

'I have two,' he said, 'both boys. And two step-daughters. What are yours?'

Tatiana knew she had lost.

'Albert, you have a very soft heart,' she said afterwards. 'She may have made up the whole story.'

'Oh, I'm sure she didn't,' he said, 'and even if she had, how could I let her go on being so miserable?'

One afternoon, during a visit to Leyden, Albert sat at home with Paul, having an absorbing scientific discussion. When the telephone rang in the next room they scarcely heard it, and it wasn't until Tatiana came running into the room, her face flushed, that they realized it *was* a telephone that had momentarily interrupted their thoughts.

'You're both to go at once to the Naval School. There's some sort of celebration on and all the Royal Family are going to be there.' Tatiana stopped for breath and her eyes fell on Albert's baggy trousers and creased jacket. 'I suppose that's all you've got to wear?'

He nodded unconcernedly. 'You know it is.'

'Oh, my goodness, what can we do? Paul has only got his own tails and they're ninety years old.'

Eventually, after countless telephone calls to friends, a borrowed suit was located for Albert, and he and Paul, who smelt faintly of mothballs, arrived at the reception.

'Now remember,' Paul whispered, 'we'll just be presented, and then we'll go home.' On the threshold their names were announced by a man in a scarlet uniform and they advanced into the crowded room to be presented to Queen Wilhelmina and to her Consort, Hendrik, and then, as they had planned, they edged their way back to the door, and had almost reached it when a Court official barred their way.

'Sirs, the Queen Mother would like to meet you.' Albert and Paul had no choice but to be escorted back into the middle of the hall.

Emma, the Queen Mother, a charming old lady who had been Regent for Wilhelmina for eight years, smiled at the fugitives.

'Did you think I did not notice that you were trying to give us the slip? I spotted you. I think you still have time to shake hands with an old lady, gentlemen.'

Albert was never awed by Royalty, and on the occasion when the University conferred an honorary doctorate on the Queen, he decided to prove to his colleagues that he could look as splendid as any of them. He was always being teased about his appearance, and since all the professors were to march in their academic caps and gowns from the University to the Town Hall and back again, he obtained a fantastic fancy dress, a silk cape that reached trailing to the ground, pale blue and adorned with gold lace, and a soft headgear rather like a beret on which flourished two large white ostrich feathers. He duly took his place in the procession, and waved and smiled at the cheering crowds. No-one ever knew if Queen Wilhelmina realized that Professor Einstein's robes were not those of some foreign university.

Although Albert's time was now divided between Holland and Germany, he was no less admired in Berlin. He was now included in the tourist sights of the city, and his lectures were open to the public. Sightseers packed the lecture hall, often regretting the enthusiasm which had drawn them there when they found they couldn't understand a word of what Albert was saying. Sometimes Albert paused and said, 'I shall stop for a short time so that anyone who wishes to leave may do so.' Usually, on these occasions, only about ten people stayed, but Albert preferred to talk to a few people who were really interested than an enormous audience whose blank faces concealed equally blank minds.

On 14th March, 1929, Albert was fifty. As the day grew near newspapers began to print promises of articles in which Albert's personal views on all sorts of matters would be revealed.

'It's going to be terrible on the day,' Elsa said, 'we won't have a moment to ourselves.'

'Honestly, father,' suggested Ilse, 'it would be better to leave Berlin altogether and come back afterwards. Quite apart from those wretched reporters, the telephone won't stop ringing.'

It was true, Albert had a great many friends and acquaintances who were bound to want to congratulate him, and all sorts of people who didn't know him but who admired him, would probably want to pay their respects too.

'We'll all go away then,' Albert said. 'After all, it is *my* birthday. I don't see why I shouldn't enjoy it.'

As soon as he left Berlin the Press got busy. 'Einstein in Holland,' said one headline. 'Albert Einstein in U.S. for Half-Century,' announced another. In fact Albert had gone into the country about an hour's journey from Berlin. He had a friend there who owned an estate, and he lent Albert a pavilion in his garden, a comfortable and ornamental building on the edge of a lake. Elsa had decided that she and the girls would stay in the flat, and go down to Albert on the morning of the 14th. She spent the previous day preparing a special lunch which she could take with her, and sorting through the letters and parcels which were already arriving in hundreds.

His actual birthday was a pleasant day for Albert. He wore his old trousers and a sweater and no shoes or socks. His beloved family were with him, and he was touched by the presents and congratulations which had come from so many sources. An American Zionist group had bought a piece of land in Palestine and planted it with trees. The woods which would in time grow there were going to be called Einstein Grove. An unemployed man sent a twist of tobacco. Some of Albert's friends had clubbed together to give him a very up-to-date sailing boat, since he had lately taken up sailing as a hobby.

Albert spent the afternoon composing a piece of not very good doggerel verse which he sent to all his friends.

> Each shows his best side to me,
> On this my anniversary.
> And my friends from far and near
> Have written charming things to hear,
> Sent me food and choicest wine,
> All a glutton could divine
> To bring contentment if they can
> To such a hoary-headed man!
> Murmuring in dulcet tone
> Things that for my age atone.
> Haughty now and almost regal
> I feel as proud as any eagle.
> But now the day draws to an end
> And I return the compliment.
> Brilliantly I think you've done,
> You've even brought a smiling sun!

There was one present which Albert had still to receive. The Berlin City Council had decided to give him a small house on the bank of the Havel River. Albert already knew about this, and, indeed, for months past there had been pictures of 'Einstein House' in newspapers and magazines.

Soon after Albert's birthday Elsa went to see the house, and was astonished to observe curtains at the windows and obvious signs of habitation — even a line of washing outside the back door. She came to the conclusion that the tenants must be leaving shortly, and decided to make sure. She approached the house and asked the maid if she could have a word with the tenant. When she explained her reason for calling, the man became extremely indignant. Certainly not, he said, the Council had bought the house but they had guaranteed him the right to remain there.

Elsa angrily reported this conversation to the Council, who were covered with confusion, and horrified that such an error should have arisen, particularly when the gift had received such publicity and concerned such an illustrious citizen.

As the park in which the house stood was a large one, they selected another part of it, a particularly delightful plot which backed on to the river, and presented this to Albert. They made it clear, however, that the house he was going to build was to be at his own expense. Albert and Elsa took this in good part, and were in fact happy to have such a beautiful site. They found an architect and had plans drawn up for a spacious yet labour-saving log-built bungalow.

'Don't let any salesman talk you into buying a lift, Albertle,' Elsa said. As his mother had done, she often used the affectionate Swabian diminutive of his name. 'You've never held out against persuasion yet.'

The building was on the point of going ahead when the second blow fell. The owner of the original house stated that not only had he acquired the right to live in it, but also the right to be the sole tenant of the park.

It was really very embarrassing, and Albert

137

E*

wished the whole affair could be dropped. But the Municipal Council was determined to go on, and after lengthy negotiations they obtained permission to give Albert a piece of the park – a rather inferior piece which wasn't even near the river. But this, which was far removed in grandeur from the initial present of a charming house, was just as disastrous. It now turned out that the Council had no right to give away any part of the park at all!

Albert said quite firmly this time that he would prefer to have no gift at all, but since everyone knew of the muddle and the Council's original gesture, it would have been too degrading for them to agree, and they insisted on finding a solution.

'You must choose a vacant plot,' they told Albert, 'and we will buy it and give it to you. Then there can be no mistake.'

Elsa went land-hunting, and after a few weeks she found an ideal spot for their bungalow in a village called Kaputh, near Potsdam. She told the Council, and at their next meeting a motion was put forward for buying it.

One of the members rose to his feet.

'Does Einstein deserve such an expensive present?' he asked. 'I think before we table the motion we should discuss it further.'

And discuss it they did, and at such length it was postponed until the next meeting. But in the meantime Albert heard about it and wrote to the Mayor of Berlin, saying that life was too short to wait for the laborious grindings of the Council's machinery. He thanked them for their intentions, but, since his birthday was over, he declined their gift.

So now Albert had not only to pay for the building of his bungalow, but for the land as well. Elsa was delighted to have a home of their own after living so long in a flat in Berlin, although practically all their savings had gone in acquiring it.

'That was the most expensive birthday present I've ever had,' said Albert.

CHAPTER SIXTEEN

The Fugitive

SINCE his visit there nearly ten years before Albert had wanted to go back to America. When he was asked to spend the three coming winters in Pasadena, California, as visiting Professor at the California Institute of Technology, he was delighted. In December he and Elsa left for the United States, spent a glorious winter in the sunshine and returned to Berlin in the spring. It was a pleasant arrangement, and Albert was very happy dividing his time between the two countries.

'More of the film-star treatment,' he said, as he went ashore on his second visit and saw the battery of photographers awaiting him. He got a real film-star reception a month later when he went to Hollywood and visited Charlie Chaplin, who had invited him to dinner and then to his private cinema to see his film, *City Lights*. As they drove to the town they were recognized by the crowds in the streets, and were cheered loudly. Charlie Chaplin turned to Albert with a smile. 'You're being cheered because nobody understands you and I'm being cheered because everybody understands me!'

Everywhere Albert went he had this kind of reception, and he tried not to be irritated by the lack of privacy. In Germany he was less of a novelty and his life was quieter, but he was far from happy at the political developments there. In 1932 there was a Presidential election, and the two opposing candidates were Paul von Hindenburg and Adolf Hitler. Hindenburg won, and appointed a Chancellor who was almost a military dictator. When Albert left for Pasadena for his third winter there, he told Elsa, 'Before you leave the bungalow take a good look at it.'

'Why?' she asked.

'Because you won't see it again.'

In January, President Hindenburg appointed a new Chancellor—his former opponent, Adolf Hitler.

It must be remembered that a President of a country is less like a Prime Minister and more like a King, and various Governments are formed under him. The policy of this new Government was that of the State's supremacy over every aspect of life. Everything—art, science, philosophy—had to serve the State. And one of the first steps the Government took to realize their policy was to sack any teacher or professor they considered 'unfit' for the post. The ones they considered unfit were Jews—even a person who had one Jewish grandparent was a 'non-Aryan' and lost his job. So did those with 'non-Aryan' wives. The Germans who had idolized Albert now began to hate him with a fierce, fanatical hatred. Not only was he rumoured to be the leader of a secret movement against the Government, but his theories were re-examined and presented as 'Jewish' and 'Bolshevist'.

'The most important example of the dangerous influence of Jewish circles on the study of nature has been provided by Herr Einstein with his mathematically botched-up theories consisting of some ancient knowledge and a few arbitrary additions'

ran one Government-sponsored newspaper article. It isn't difficult to make unthinking people believe what they read – especially when the same arguments appear in a number of places.

Albert decided he would not return to Berlin, and when he left Pasadena he went to a Belgian seaside resort, Le Coque. When he arrived he wrote to the Academy in Berlin resigning his post, and they publicly accepted his resignation.

'Can't we go back home?' Elsa asked longingly. 'Even if it is only to sell the house and pack up our belongings.'

'If we did go back we would never be allowed to leave,' Albert answered. And as if to prove his words he received news that his bungalow at Kaputh had been searched, his property confiscated, his honorary citizenship renounced and his written work burned with the work of other Jewish writers, publicly, in a huge bonfire in front of the

State Opera House in Berlin. There was also a warrant out for his arrest, and a huge reward for his capture.

They stayed in Le Coque until the autumn. Here, in this picturesque seaside town Albert lived very quietly. Every week he played his violin with a group of musicians which included the talented Queen of the Belgians. His house was on the front, and the gaiety of the holiday-makers, the children building castles, eating ice-creams, running races barefoot along the sands, did nothing to lighten his sense of depression and foreboding.

'My greatest fear is that this hate and power epidemic will spread throughout the world,' he wrote in a letter to a friend.

Albert's fears were not for himself but for humanity, yet he had good reason to be afraid. Le Coque was near the German border and it would have been a simple expedition for a German 'patriot' to come into Belgium and kill him – and with such a high reward offered it was a likely possibility. So likely, in fact, that the Belgian Government and Royal Family thought it wise to give Albert a body-guard, and two powerfully built, crack-shot men were sent to his villa to watch him day and night. Albert found it extremely irksome and constantly complained he was under 'police supervision'.

When a friend, Philipp Frank, who had been his successor in Prague, came to visit him, and found his way – in spite of security measures – to Albert's house, the bodyguards leapt on him and led him to the house, where Elsa fortunately recognized and identified him. But no real assassins made the attempt, although there was one strange and unpleasant incident. A letter came from a German Albert did not know. He asked Albert to see him, and when Albert refused, followed the first letter with such a bombardment of others that Elsa decided she would meet him and find out what the man wanted.

He arrived at their meeting-place, and told Elsa he was an ex-Nazi Storm-trooper, and now wanted to sell all the party secrets to Albert.

Elsa looked at him, astonished. 'Why do you think my husband would spend all that money on your party's secrets?'

'Because everyone knows that Professor Einstein leads the opposing party throughout the world.'

Elsa assured the German that this was an error, but it was disturbing to know that the Nazis believed Albert to be the leader of an opposition political party – all the more reason for them to make sure his life was not prolonged.

Albert did not intend to stay long in Belgium. He considered going to Paris or Spain, where he had been offered posts, or to America, or even to Jerusalem where he could work in the university his efforts had helped to build. But although the authorities were anxious to have him there, Albert felt it was far better for a young Jewish scientist already in Palestine to take the post than someone like himself, already famous and now, suddenly, free. He was, nevertheless, seriously concerned with the thousands of Jewish scholars who were being expelled from Germany. He visited London where an Academic Assistance Council had been formed to aid these refugees, and spoke on 'Science and Liberty' at a meeting at the Albert Hall. As he stepped on to the platform the vast audience of seven thousand people spontaneously stood up to greet him.

From England, together with Elsa, Margot and his secretary, Helen Dukas, Albert went to America, where he had finally decided to live. He was particularly interested in the Institute for Advanced Studies in Princeton, a newly-formed institution devoted entirely to research, and having no prejudices, racial, political or national. A Negro, a Buddhist, a Chinese, an Indian – man or woman – could work there provided they merited the job. Albert supported this basic principle wholeheartedly, and the founder, Dr. Flexner, had approached him the previous winter in Pasadena. They had met again at Christ Church in Oxford, where Albert was staying to give a lecture, and there, in the peaceful and beautiful English college garden, the spires outlined against the pale evening sky, Dr. Flexner had said simply, 'Professor Einstein, I would not presume to offer you a post in this new institution, but if on reflection you decide that it would afford you the opportunity which you value, you would be welcome on your own terms.'

Even before Albert left Berlin he had intended to

spend some part of each year in Princeton, as he had done in Pasadena. Now he decided to go there permanently.

Elsa found a house with a large garden, a mile and a half from the Institute, and Albert often used to walk to work along the pleasant suburban avenue. His room at the Institute was large and completely quiet, and he continued with his research as if he had never been uprooted. He loved America and did not feel in the least homesick. But Elsa was not so adaptable. She never really accepted that she was living in America, not merely visiting, and even the summer holiday they spent in a beautiful old house near the mouth of the Connecticut River did not make her have any less longing for Kaputh and the Havel.

It was her last holiday. In 1936 she became suddenly ill and died, and without her Albert felt that all his links with Germany were severed. It was a sad year of loss for him, for both his stepdaughter Ilse and his old friend from Zürich, Marcel Grossmann, died too. He continued to live in his house in Princeton, and Margot and Helen Dukas looked after him. Helen, like himself and Elsa, came originally from Swabia. He was immersed in his work, but not too involved to be unaware of the approaching war. In 1938 Germany invaded Czechoslovakia. In 1939 it was Poland, and England declared war. In 1939, too, as a result of a conference with physicists from Columbia University, Albert wrote a letter to President Roosevelt.

'Some recent work' his letter began —'which has been communicated to me in manuscript, leads me to expect that the element of uranium may be turned into a new and important source of energy in the immediate future — that extremely powerful bombs of a new type may thus be contructed.'

It was, of course, the atom bomb, and Albert was aware that while America had little source of uranium, Germany had a great deal, and might well produce such a bomb. Albert advised the President on the necessity of special research on nuclear fission in the United States. America was not yet at war, but she was supporting the Allies in every possible way. Albert knew that his own early discovery in the field of atomic energy had resulted nearly forty years later in a terrible threat of devastation, and by suggesting to President Roosevelt that America should work urgently to produce an atomic weapon he had put himself in a position of frightening responsibility. He was convinced that if he had not pioneered the way some other physicist would have reached the same conclusion before very long, and although he was a pacifist he believed that men should fight for freedom when freedom was truly threatened as it was now. And Science, in 1939, was an integral part of warfare.

CHAPTER SEVENTEEN

American Citizen

F OR many years now Maja and Paul had lived in
Florence, but when Italy began to fall under
Nazi influence Maja felt she would be happier – and
safer – somewhere else. Naturally her thoughts
turned to Albert in America. Now that both their
parents were dead and there were no ties left to keep
her in Europe she felt she would like to be with her
brother again. Paul went to Switzerland, and Maja
travelled to Princeton, officially as a visitor, but
determined to stay for good.

Albert was overjoyed to see her, and with the
prospect of having her as a near neighbour he
helped her with all the immigration formalities, and
to find a home and work for Paul. He was an old
hand at solving such problems. He had become a
symbolic leader for the Jewish refugees who were
now pouring into America. He was like a father to
them, never refusing to give advice, sending books,
letters, recommendations, whenever he was asked.
It was particularly the young scholars who turned to

him. He was a Jew of international fame and prestige who had worked for the Zionist cause, and they felt if he could not help them plant new roots, no-one else would. His efforts made him unpopular among certain people. It was levelled against him that when he helped a refugee to find a job he was at the same time preventing an American from working. Rumours were spread that these foreign Jews wanted to get rich without hard work or to live on charity. Albert himself gave two violin recitals in New York and presented the large sums of money they raised to refugee causes.

He became an American citizen in 1941 and in his new country he was now something of a myth. A schoolgirl wrote him a letter asking if he was really a person or a kind of fairy story. It made Albert a rather solitary person. All he had done as a scientist and a Jew had made him legendary to the world at large. Everything he did or said was magnified and given importance.

'I have become a lonely old fellow,' he wrote to a friend in Palestine, 'a kind of patriarchal figure who is known chiefly because he does not wear socks.'

It was refreshing when he met a person who had not heard of him. Once, at a dinner party, he sat next to a pretty teen-age girl who was still at school.

'What are you by profession?' she asked Albert innocently.

'I devote myself to the study of physics,' Albert said without sarcasm.

The girl looked at him in amazement. 'You mean

to say you study physics at your age?' she said. 'I
finished mine a year ago.'

Usually it was only children who treated Albert
unaffectedly these days. A little girl, the daughter
of a neighbour in Princeton, had heard that the kind-
looking man with the long white hair who lived up
the road was very clever with arithmetic. She became stuck with her homework one week-end, and
decided that he was the man to help her. She gathered up her books and walked down the street to
Albert's house. He answered the door himself.

'I heard you are good at sums,' she said, 'and I
wondered if you could show me how to do my
homework?'

'Come in,' said Albert at once, 'I'm sure I can.'

When the girl's mother found out what had
happened she was embarrassed and upset, and
personally called on Albert to apologize.

'Please,' Albert assured her, 'you don't have to be
sorry. I enjoyed myself, and learned more from her
than she did from me. She can come any time she
likes.'

* * *

In the same year, 1939, that Maja and Paul came to
live in Princeton, the World's Fair opened in New
York. Every country was represented by splendidly
designed pavilions, built to house their produce
and art and machinery. Palestine was among them.
As each pavilion was opened, the ambassador of
the country gave an address, and it was unani-
mously decided that although Albert was not the

ambassador he must open the Palestine pavilion. It was as if someone had at last tied a label round his neck saying officially what had been generally known for a long time—*Einstein, leader of the Jews*.

In 1941 the Japanese suddenly bombed the American Fleet at Pearl Harbour, thus bringing the United States actively into the war. In 1945 an atom bomb was dropped on Hiroshima in Japan. Albert, fully conscious of the part he himself had played, was horrified at the misery and devastation the bomb had caused, but at the same time relieved beyond measure that by taking this step America had possibly prevented years of further suffering. The war was now over. Events had made it imperative for the United States to develop and use the bomb. Now there was only one thing left to do. The secret of its manufacture must be kept and never used again. There was no defence against such a weapon. The world must be taught that harmonious living between countries was the only guarantee for peace, that there must be mutual trust and no war. If scientists could make this clear to all Governments, then their part in creating the atom bomb would be atoned for. New and lasting foundations would be built from the destruction.

'I do hope,' Albert said to Maja a few days after peace had been declared, 'that fear of atomic warfare will make people think twice before they become too nationalistic.'

* * *

Albert had not been well for some time. His heart

was bad and his doctors in Princeton had sent him to Brooklyn to the Jewish hospital there to have an operation to diagnose the exact trouble.

The diagnosis was not a happy one. There was no cure. Albert might die at any time. No-one could say how long he had left, it could be six months or six years. Professor Nissen, who had performed the operation, had the unpleasant task of telling Albert the opinion of his doctors. But Albert was not in the least perturbed.

'I enjoy life,' he said, 'at times it's marvellous. But honestly, if you told me I had only three hours to live I shouldn't worry. I'd spend the time putting my papers in order.'

He went back to work happily, but it had not occurred to him that he would outlive Maja. He was deeply upset when after an illness she died in 1951, and in a letter to Lisbeth Hurwitz, the daughter of his old friend and one-time mathematics teacher, he wrote in a sad way, unlike his usual cheerful self.

'Personally I am fairly well,' he said, 'even if my old machinery has started to rattle a bit. I have given up the violin for some years now. I am certain you remember the Bach and Handel Sonatas we played with such pleasure under the skilful leadership of your father. Think of it, it was nearly forty years ago!'

Forty years ago! Albert had not dreamed then of the public life before him. Then he was a physicist in Zürich, newly appointed professor at the University. Now he was an old man whose name was known and respected all over the world. He was under no illusion about this. How could he be, when everywhere he went he was treated with reverence and awe? But the honour that was paid to him in 1952 was one he had never anticipated. In 1948 Britain had given up her Mandate for Palestine, and a new nation, Israel, had come into being. Albert's old friend Chaim Weizmann was the first President. He died on November 9th. Who would be the new Head of the State of Israel? A Tel-Aviv newspaper supported Albert Einstein, and the suggestion was taken up by the *New York Times*. The Israeli Ambassador, Mr. Abba Eban, telephoned to Washington to talk to Albert, and Jews everywhere waited breathlessly to learn what Albert had replied.

'I have never taken any job for which I am unsuited,' he said simply to the Ambassador. And later he composed an official letter of refusal.

'I am deeply moved by the offer of our State of Israel,' he wrote. 'Naturally I am also sad and ashamed that it is impossible for me to accept this offer. Having been busied with objective things throughout my life, I have neither the capacity nor the experience in the correct handling of men and the practise of official functions. I would be quite unable to fulfil this high task because my advanced age has considerably reduced my strength. This undeniable fact makes me even sadder because my relationship to the Jewish people has become my strongest human bond, since I am fully aware of our precarious situation among the other races.'

It was a plain and moving reply to the greatest tribute his people could have paid.

Tributes of all kinds were never lacking, and some of them were equally unexpected. On his seventy-fourth birthday the Cake Bakers' Union of New York presented him with a cake made in the shape of a book on a lectern stand. *Happy Birthday Professor Albert Einstein* was written in chocolate on the open marzipan page. The cake was so elaborate – covered with icing-sugar flowers, red roses, blue forget-me-nots, purple violets – and so large, that it took two men to lift it from the van in which it arrived at Albert's home.

In spite of the doctor's gloomy prophecy, Albert was still tolerably well and able to enjoy his birthday. He was still able to fight for a worthy cause too, and the following year he again found it necessary to attack intolerance and oppression. A nuclear physicist, Robert Oppenheimer, Director of the Institute of Advanced Studies and a man Albert knew well and respected, was dismissed from his post because it was believed he held Communist sympathies.

Old age and ill health were not going to stop Albert speaking his mind, and with the clarity and forcefulness of a young man he defended his colleague.

* * *

Albert's last birthday was in 1955. In April he signed an appeal sent to him by the English philosopher, Bertrand Russell, entreating Governments to renounce nuclear war, and signed by eminent scientists from all parts of the world including Professor Joliot-Curie, Marie Curie's son-in-law, who had married Eve.

'Most of us are not neutral in feeling,' it said, 'but as human beings, we have to remember that, if the issues between East and West are to be decided in any manner that can give any possible satisfaction to anybody, whether Communist or anti-Communist, whether Asian or European or American, whether White or Black, then these issues must not be decided by war.'

All his life Albert had supported principles like this one.

When the recent supply of Russian and Czech arms to Egypt had made Israel's position very insecure, Einstein offered to explain Israel's point of view through the medium of American radio and television. The respective networks were enthusiastic about the suggestion, which was to be put into effect on April 27, Israel Independence Day. But a few days before Albert became ill. He was taken to Princeton Hospital, where he refused an operation, knowing it would do little good. But the treatment he had there relieved his pain and he felt well enough to work. Within a few hours he had telephoned his secretary to bring his glasses and papers to the hospital, and asked to see Margot, who was in a neighbouring ward for some minor illness. She arrived in a wheelchair.

'How elegantly you rode into the room,' joked Albert.

Over the week-end he felt even better, and was delighted to see his son, Albert, who had flown from Berkeley, where he was now working as an engineer. On Sunday night it seemed as if he would, after all, recover. He was cheerful and alert, and when he turned out the light to sleep, his unfinished work which he intended to complete tomorrow, was on the bedside table. At midnight he was sleeping peacefully. At one o'clock, quite suddenly, his heart stopped beating.

*　　*　　*

There was no public funeral. Albert had expressly wished it. He would have liked to have given his body for medical research but he knew that it would have been interpreted by the world as a theatrical gesture. He wanted no acclaim, or monuments, or vast weeping crowds. He was not a film-star idol. If he had worked hard and done good and useful things it was because he had wanted to do so, not for any effect it might create.

He was cremated on the day he died, and only his closest friends and relatives were there for the ceremony.

'Here on earth I have done my job,' he had said to Margot a few days before. And three months later, when the scientists' appeal for peace was released to the world's Press, with Albert's name posthumously among the signatures, it was apparent that the ideas he believed in and fought for had not died with him.

Einstein's Scientific Work

A Note by

M. A. JASWON, M.A., PH.D.

Ever since the dawn of history, thousands of years ago, men have been fascinated by the heavenly bodies. The sun dominates our lives, rising and setting every day with perfect regularity. Next in importance comes the moon, ruler of the night sky, going through its well-known cycle of appearance every month. Then there are the planets, including this earth of ours, which revolve in orbits round the sun. Finally, the fixed stars form worlds of their own at unimaginable distances away. Many references to the heavenly bodies occur in the Bible, showing very clearly the great impression they made on the ancient Hebrews. It was left, however, to another distinguished people of antiquity, the Greeks, to provide descriptions of the way in which the planets moved. These descriptions were largely incorrect, and often fanciful, but all the same made the beginnings of a scientific outlook. So great was the fame of the Greek astronomer Ptolemy of Alexandria, that his system was accepted without question over the whole of Europe till about the beginning of the 17th century. By that time, improved instruments of observation, and methods of calculation, had convinced educated men, much to their regret, that the Greek picture could not be true.

The modern scientific era may be said to have begun in the year 1687, when Sir Isaac Newton introduced the idea of a force, termed gravity, acting throughout the entire Universe. If we throw a stone into the air, it always falls back again to the ground. Common sense tells us, or seems to tell us, that there must be a force at the centre of the earth which attracts all objects towards it. This is gravity. It is gravity which keeps everybody earthbound; it is gravity which keeps the planets circling round the sun; it is gravity which must be fought against when sputniks and rockets are hurtled into space. By recognizing the existence of gravity men have calculated the paths of the heavenly bodies to an extraordinary degree of accuracy, making it possible to predict eclipses of the sun and moon, to understand the whole rhythm of the skies, to prepare the calendar for years in advance, and to anticipate the appearance of comets. The story is told that Sir Isaac Newton came to the idea of gravity because of an apple, which fell off a tree and struck his head while he was dozing in the garden. He at once asked himself: why did the apple fall down and not just stay where it was? From this simple beginning, his wonderful idea was born.

A remarkable test of Newton's theory came in the year 1845. It had been noticed by astronomers that the planet Uranus, in circling round the sun, did not exactly follow the path expected. To what could this be due? Two mathematicians, Adams in England and, independently, Leverrier in France, studied the problem and came to a most significant conclusion. They said there existed a planet, unknown to all the astronomers, which was passing close to Uranus and affecting its behaviour. Furthermore, they predicted the size and shape of the unknown planet, which they called Neptune, and the position it should occupy in the heavens. A few months later, Neptune was observed at the precise position indicated by Adams and Leverrier, and from that day to this has taken its place as a planet together with all the others.

By virtue of its great successes, Newton's scheme of things reigned supreme for over 200 years. Finally, however, at the beginning of the present century, it was challenged (as you have read in this book) by Albert Einstein. What were the grounds for his attitude? Gravity certainly provided a good working description of nature, but his enquiring mind was not satisfied. How did this force come to exist, and by what means did it exert its action between bodies? Unless these fundamental questions could be answered, the whole thing remained for him a mystery. After years of deep study and reflection, Einstein at last came forward with his answer. It involved nothing less than a complete change in the way we must picture the world. New points of view are always difficult to understand and accept, and Einstein's was no exception. Eventually, however, its power, beauty and value became recognized, and it has become accepted by all physical scientists as one of the grandest creations of the century.

A very clear model of Relativity, as the new theory was called, has been introduced by the celebrated English scientist Sir Arthur Eddington. Suppose we were to regard the earth as flat, as in the days before Columbus, and on this basis tried to work out the best route for a ship sailing from London to New York. We would take a map of the earth, and on this map draw a straight line joining the two cities. If the flat-earth picture were correct, this would indeed be the route required. In practice, however, experienced sailors would soon notice that the best route in fact was not a straight line, but a curved line bending towards the North. How would this curious and unexpected fact be explained by scientists holding the flat-earth picture? They would say that obviously there existed a force at the North Pole, which attracted all moving objects to the North. In due course, this wrong theory would then become accepted by everybody because it seemed to fit the facts of the situation.

Every schoolchild knows full well why the best route is not a straight line. It has nothing whatever to do with mysterious forces coming from the North Pole. For the earth is round, not flat, and ships must therefore travel on arcs of circles in moving from one point of the globe to another; when projected on to a map, these arcs of circles appear as curved lines, not as straight lines. Thus, by forming a correct picture of the earth, the whole mystery of the curved lines on the map is explained in a most natural manner. In a very similar way, Einstein suggested that our whole picture of space and time required altering, but only a mathematician can fully understand this. By adopting these new ideas, gravity is seen in an entirely new light, and all the difficulties about it are removed. For most practical applications, Einstein's theory yields the same results as that of Newton, but has proved to be superior in certain delicate tests. For this reason, we still make use of gravity in ordinary practical life, and only dispense with it as our scientific studies get more advanced.

Besides Relativity, Einstein made several other important contributions to physical science. In the year 1905, when he was only 25 years old, he put forward revolutionary new ideas on the nature of light, of electricity, and of molecular motion. All these have stood the test of time, and indeed are now regarded as the foundation stones of modern physics. Any one of these contributions alone would have established the reputation of an ordinary scientist. As it has turned out, however, they are completely overshadowed by the Theory of Relativity, which came ten years later, and with which Einstein's name will always be associated.